Television
Here is the news
Anthony Davis

Television
Here is the news
Anthony Davis

SEVERN HOUSE PUBLISHERS

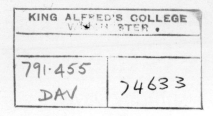
Severn House Publishers Ltd
144–146 New Bond Street
London W.1.
with grateful acknowledgement to the
co-operation of
Independent Television Publications Ltd

© Anthony Davis 1976

ISBN: 0 7278 0168 6

Filmset in 'Monophoto' Times 10 on 11 pt by
Richard Clay (The Chaucer Press), Ltd, Bungay, Suffolk
and printed in Great Britain by
Fletcher & Son Ltd, Norwich

Contents

Foreword

By Sir Geoffrey Cox

Television has had a great impact on journalism. The twenty years since television got properly into its stride in Britain have seen the television screen replace the newspapers and radio as the main source of news for most people in this country. The same has been true in many countries abroad, particularly in the United States. The capacity of television to enable people to 'see it as it happens' – to quote an early ITN slogan – has been powerful indeed. Nor is this impact surprising. A news medium which can enable millions of people to see man setting foot onto the surface of the moon at the very moment when it is occurring is a medium which print or the spoken word can challenge only with difficulty.

The development of television news has been swift, vivid and constantly changing. This book sets out the main lines of that story as it has unfolded in Britain. For those who as journalists have had the good fortune to have been caught up in this historic process, the story stirs many memories and many emotions. For all viewers it provides an insight into the complex process which turns news into television, that daily technical miracle which gathers up the news in pictures from the four corners of the world, and, nightly, without fuss presents it to us in our sitting rooms. It is the story of a journalistic revolution – and of a revolution as yet unfinished.

Geoffrey Cox

Preface

A crisis, a disaster, any happening of importance anywhere in the world, and television's news organizations will bring the story and pictures swiftly to the living-room screen. Current affairs programmes will back up the bulletins with more detailed reports, interpretation and discussion, viewers having their own favourites among the newscasters, reporters and interviewers. All this is taken for granted now, since the majority of people have for some years relied on television for most of their news and information, and 'the news' enjoys a high measure of trust. It is possibly the most respected part of the television service, though it is not left uncriticized. For example, it has been attacked for concentrating on action and personalities rather than issues and explanation.

This day-to-day news service has come about within two decades. Before 1955 journalism was regarded as belonging to radio and the press, television being primarily a medium of entertainment. Today television is theatre and newspaper in one. Routine newscasts reach more people than even the most popular newspapers, and while generally television drama, comedy and light entertainment shows draw the biggest audiences, news programmes at the time of a general election, a royal occasion or an event such as a space mission can win even bigger ones.

This book sets out to tell the story of how news and current affairs came to television and of major events in their development, of the men and women in the field and in the studio who bring the programmes to the screen, and of the pressures and problems they face. My thanks are due to all those in television journalism who gave generously of their time to help me in the writing of it.

A. D.

Chapter 1

News comes to television

Television news as we know it today began at 10 pm on 22 September 1955, ITV's opening night in London, when Christopher Chataway, a copper-haired twenty-four-year-old, well known to the public as an Olympic runner, introduced the first ITN newscast. Its personal style of presentation, colloquial language and extensive use of film contrasted dramatically with the formal bulletins delivered in measured tones on BBC Television. Until eighteen days earlier (by which time ITN's plans were public knowledge) BBC newsreaders had been heard but not seen and BBC news had been authoritative but dull.

Until 1954 there had been no television news programmes at all, other than outside broadcasts of major events, such as the Coronation (about which more later) and newsreels, which could be interesting and informative but had little to do with the big news of the day on which they were shown.

The early days

When television began in Britain as the world's first regular high-definition service on 2 November 1936 it showed the newsreels of Gaumont-British and British Movietone, the very same as those that could be seen at the cinemas. At that time there were just two hours of television a day, one in the afternoon and one in the evening, and there were only four hundred sets capable of receiving the service, all of them inevitably in the London area, because the sole transmitter was in London. Television's budget was tiny; its function to amuse.

On 1 September 1939 television closed down for the duration of the war in case German bombers should home in on the transmitter. After its return on 7 June 1946 it spread slowly across the country, but, for the first eight post-war years, news still meant only outside broadcasts and newsreels. In 1948 the BBC progressed to making its own newsreels which, from weekly editions with repeats, became bi-weekly and eventually nightly ones, but they remained leisurely and insular. As a BBC publication of 1950, Frank Tilsley's *Television Story*, said, they ranged 'from the week's sport to scenes at a dock strike, from the Open Air Theatre at Regent's Park to tractors harvesting the season's wheat'. That they did not cover all the major happenings of the preceding hours was hardly surprising. When the BBC thought of

BBC Newsreel *cameraman filming a television garden party in the Alexandra Palace grounds in 1949*

news it thought of radio. It had been in radio a long time and radio was the medium for immediacy; film took time to shoot and to process and edit, and there was no competition to encourage speed of presentation. Lord Simon of Wythenshawe, Chairman of the BBC Board of Governors from 1947 to 1952, summed up the Corporation attitude in these words:

> A great majority of [news] items are of such a nature that they cannot, either now or ever, be shown visually; of those that could be shown on television the majority occur overseas, often in distant countries, and it will be a long time before television films can be flown from all over the world to London on the day on which they happen. Television newsreels will, of course, continue to develop and be of the greatest interest and attraction, but there is surely not the least possibility that they will ever replace the news on sound.*

This was the general feeling of television men, journalists and the public, for satellite communications were still science-fiction fantasies. But in 1954, with the impetus given to the sale of television sets by the coronation coverage, and the knowledge that ITV would soon be providing competition, the BBC began *Television News and Newsreel*, heralded as 'a service of the greatest significance in the progress of

* *The BBC from Within* (London: Gollancz 1953), p. 138.

television in the UK'. In fact, it was a nightly ten minutes consisting of a reading of the latest radio news to an accompaniment of still pictures, followed by the familiar newsreel. A BBC statement said:

News and Newsreel . . . aims at giving the public in the UK as comprehensive an illustrated service of news as is possible within the limitations imposed by the existing sources of illustration and their availability. It is hoped that eventually this service will be the equal in scope of that which has been given in sound for many years. The Corporation intends to secure world-wide sources of news in pictures, rather in the same way that it has secured sources in words. Eventually perhaps there will be little more delay in receiving moving pictures of happenings in some parts of the world than there now is in getting words. The full potentialities of televising in this field are only just beginning to suggest themselves.

BBC Television, which had been housed since 1936 in Alexandra Palace in North London, now moved to new studios at Shepherd's Bush in West London, but retained the Palace to be its first television news centre under the editorship of Pat Smithers, a former Fleet Street and radio journalist. However, the newsreaders were still radio men based at Broadcasting House and they took it in turn to trek out to Alexandra Palace – 'Ally Pally' – to read the news for television. The first among these was Richard Baker, who introduced the first *News and Newsreel* at 7.30 pm on 5 July 1954 with these words: 'Here is an illustrated summary of the news. It will be followed by the latest film of events and happenings at home and abroad.' He was not seen by viewers – and nor was John Snagge who followed him, reading a report on truce talks in Indo-China. On the screen a newsreel-type caption was followed by a map of Indo-China and then a still photograph. Another caption then introduced a story about parliamentary questions on the high price of meat. All the news was treated in this way. The film that followed in the newsreel section was of a conference of doctors, shot silent and given a background of music. Sound equipment was too heavy to be easily portable and so film, which was sometimes several days old when it reached the screen, was always backed in the studio with appropriate mood music. Gerald Barry commented in his television column in *The Observer*: 'The sad fact has to be recorded that news on television does not exist. What has been introduced nightly into the TV programmes is a perfunctory little bulletin of news flashes composed of an announcer's voice, a caption and an indifferent still photograph. This may conceivably pass as news, but it does not begin to be television.'

Even when still pictures began to yield to film the programme was little more than illustrated radio. The BBC was still conscious of its wartime role as the voice of Britain and its responsibility weighed heavily upon it. The policy laid down by the BBC for television news declared: 'The object is to state the news of the day accurately, fairly, soberly and impersonally. It is no part of the aim to induce either optimism or pessimism or to attract listeners by colourful and sensational reports. The legitimate urge to be "first with the news" must invariably be subjugated to the prior claims of accuracy.'

These instructions were enforced religiously by the head of all BBC news services, a New Zealander named Tahu Hole. No story was broadcast unless and until it had been received from two independent sources—there were no scoops on television. Staff were urged always to aim their reports at the readers of the quality press, so stories had all the colour and verve of official communiqués. Precedence was given automatically to the doings, however unimportant, of royalty, and statesmen were interviewed respectfully as they passed through London airport and invited to make statements. That their statements generally had no news value was unimportant; it was enough that eminent persons had agreed to appear on television. Newsreaders were kept out of vision to avoid any hint of personality colouring the news, though after a time it was decided to show the principal correspondents. Some, such as E. R. Thompson, the political correspondent, were natural television performers. Others were less successful. There were no teleprompters then, so their eyes flickered between their scripts and the camera lens, which made them appear furtive. One caption to a newspaper picture described them succinctly as 'the guilty men'. Leonard Parkin remembers, as a radio reporter seconded to the new service, being reprimanded for referring in a report to 'a mere two hundred people'. His use of the word 'mere' was held to be introducing an opinion, which was the worst of crimes. Another reporter recalled being told by a senior colleague, 'There is no harm in being dull.'

The emergence of Independent Television News in this constrained atmosphere had therefore considerable impact.

ITN arrives

ITN, created to serve ITV with national news, started with one great advantage: it had no history, no tradition, and therefore no preconceived ideas. It seemed logical to ITN that the emphasis of television news should be visual and that it should interest the greatest possible number of people. Its principal architect was its editor-in-chief, Aidan Crawley. When ITN began he was forty-seven. Educated at Harrow and Oxford, he had been a journalist, a producer of educational films, an RAF officer and a Labour MP. He had studied how news was handled on American television and he borrowed from this experience, adding ideas of his own. Crawley told the press that, in contrast

Aidan Crawley, first editor of ITN

to the BBC newsreaders, ITN would have news*casters*. They would be journalists, not reading-machines. They would share in the writing and compiling of the news, by taking news items and adapting them in such a way that they could relate them with natural fluency. They would be chosen for their personality and project a friendly, human manner, very different from the aloof and impersonal characteristics associated with BBC newsreaders. 'News is human and alive and we intend to present it in that manner,' declared Aidan Crawley.

Crawley chose the first newscasters from 150 candidates. There were three news programmes every weekday, from Monday to Friday and two daily at week-ends. Boldly, Crawley handed the task of presenting the noon news to a woman, Barbara Mandell, who had been a newspaper and radio reporter in South Africa and had freelanced for the BBC's *Television Newsreel*. The 7 pm programme was handled by Robin Day, a thirty-one-year-old barrister who had been briefly a producer of radio talks at the BBC. He was the most controversial choice, because he wore heavy horn-rimmed spectacles and was inclined to frown, and many of his colleagues thought him unphotogenic. The 10 pm news was presented by Chris Chataway,

Robin Day – in conventional tie – as ITN newscaster

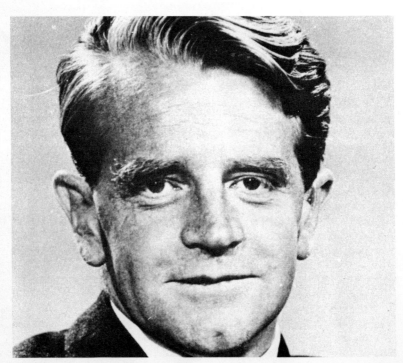

Chris Chataway – runner turned newscaster

whose public appeal was undoubted, and the week-end bulletins were shared between David Lloyd James and Rex Keating. Each programme was thus identified with a different person with an individual style.

The newscasters were seen throughout the programmes, introducing stories, interviewing and reporting. They were not the only innovation. While the BBC at that time had seemed as much a part of the Establishment as *The Times*, in contrast ITN set out to woo viewers by the same methods that the *Daily Mirror* used to attract readers. It pursued 'scoops' and 'beats' (exclusives and first disclosures). And from the beginning it used exclusively 16-mm cameras in place of the bulky 35-mm equipment of the newsreels – its films were not required to have studio quality but they had to have impact. On Crawley's instructions ITN reporters put direct and pointed questions to politicians and, if the questions were evaded, persisted until they were answered, a development which startled viewers nearly as much as the politicians themselves. They also sought the views of the man in the street on questions of the day in street-corner interviews, or 'vox pops' as they have become known by television people. Reporters were

Seeking the views of the public – a woman is interviewed about male sterilisation

encouraged to be enterprising. At an open-air strike meeting in Liverpool, Reginald Bosanquet, who had been hired fresh from university as a sub-editor, climbed on to a platform to interview Ted Hill, the boilermakers' leader, in front of three thousand shouting strikers. Again, when Norman Dodds, a Labour MP, accused work-men of laziness, citing the tea-breaks of men laying a cable outside his home, ITN took Dodds to the shelter where the men made tea for a confrontation with them. And when a workman was sent to Coventry by his colleagues in a union squabble ITN filmed his pretty young wife, who was seen declaring, 'I'll stand by my man and I don't care what they say or do.' In similar quests for spontaneity ITN followed the Housing Minister on a tour of East End slums and interpreted the 'Keep Death off the Roads' campaign by interviewing the Minister of Transport on a main road to the coast before the Whitsun rush. It covered crime stories too: its opening bulletin dealt with Jack Spot, a self-styled underworld leader, whereas the BBC had rarely touched on such subjects.

Differences between BBC and ITN coverage were typified by their treatments of a strike at the British Motor Corporation in Birmingham in July 1956. The *TV Mirror* reported:

> The BBC treated the subject with scrupulous fairness. A few brief newsreel shots were supplemented by long, carefully modified verbal reports of what the people involved had said and what the man-agement and unions were going to do. Factual, but to the great majority of people, dull.

> The ITN version consisted largely of lively, gripping film shots of the picket lines outside the factories (the part which, let's face it, had the greatest appeal for the mass of the public) backed by a simple, lucid commentary giving the main facts.

ITN brought humour to the news too. A feature of its programmes was the tailpiece delivered by the newscaster, for example: 'In Israel a car taking an expectant mother to a maternity hospital collided with a stork. An hour later the mother gave birth to a healthy boy. The stork was stunned and slightly injured. Latest reports say that it is doing as well as can be expected.' In a similar vein was this brief anecdote: 'At a music festival in Chelmsford, 350 members of a women's institute were told, "Sing like you've never sung before – raise the roof if you like". They did – and part of the roof fell in!'

All this is commonplace enough today, but it needed the pioneering spirit of the early days of ITN to establish it. Those were exhilarating days for the staff, as small and keen as it was young, and not only newscasters went out as reporters; sub-editors employed to check, cut and adapt stories to the required style and length, were also sent out to report. A commentary writer, whose job was to write the script to accompany a piece of film, could find himself 'voicing' it during the bulletin. 'This is the covered wagon era of TV news in Britain, but we believe we will make it all right,' declared Arthur Clifford, a twenty-nine-year-old news organizer who was responsible for many of the brightest ideas for the treatment of news.

But Crawley, who had brought about a revolution, was not to remain long in charge. In January 1956 he resigned after a dispute with ITN's board involving the budget and the time available to ITN and his desire to expand into current affairs programmes. The ITV programme companies, which jointly owned ITN, were losing money fast at this time; contracts were not yet licences to print money and they wanted economies.

ITN brought the Crawley-initiated style to bear on its own development. On the night Crawley resigned, the Independent Television Authority's chairman, Sir Kenneth (now Lord) Clark, was interviewed on ITN by Robin Day and the public had the unprecedented experience of seeing the chairman of an organization being cross-examined by one of the staff it controlled. It was the first live interview Day had conducted. He sought Kenneth Clark's views on the place in television of the news and whether the programme companies were the right people to control it, and extracted this statement from Sir Kenneth: 'The Authority believes that a full and responsible news service of at least twenty minutes a day is essential.' Some of the fears of the staff that the news would be abridged were allayed and Day achieved stature in the eyes of his colleagues and of the public.

Aidan Crawley was succeeded by Geoffrey Cox, a New Zealander who had been a reporter on the *Daily Express* and *News Chronicle* in the thirties, had covered the Spanish Civil War and the Finnish War, and had fought with the Eighth Army before returning to the *News Chronicle* as political correspondent and assistant editor. He relished the sense of adventure and the informality he found at ITN, and set about sustaining these while at the same time developing ITN into a major news service. Cox felt, rightly, that ITN had caught the public's attention; his task was to gain their trust in its reliability. 'We had won the first round with the BBC,' he says, 'but I knew there were many hard rounds yet to come.'

The task was not easy. Not only had the budget been cut: the editorial staff had been reduced to a total of twenty and Christopher Chataway, who had come to represent ITN to the viewers, had resigned with Crawley. Ludovic Kennedy replaced him and he and Robin Day developed into a well-matched, highly individual newscasting team. To offset the shortage of reporters, Cox had the cameras

Soviet tanks in Budapest to quell the Hungarian uprising

used more intensively, as direct reporting instruments. This led to the
new technique of recording the natural sound as well as the picture of
events, which gave a greater authenticity than the traditional newsreel
practice of silent coverage backed by music.

By the end of 1956 ITN had established the blend of hard news
reporting tempered by humour and humanity that has been its style
ever since. There had been two of the biggest stories of the post-war
period, Suez and Hungary, and in its treatment of these events ITN
won the public's trust. It was set on the road which, in the twelve years
of Cox's editorship, was to take it from being a lively and imaginative
television service into one of the most important news organs in the
country.

The BBC was following ITN's lead. Two weeks before the start of
ITN the BBC had dropped its *News and Newsreel*, replacing it with a
fifteen-minute illustrated news bulletin and moving the newsreel to a
different time. It had begun showing its newsreaders in vision,
although still anonymously and at first only during the headlines. Not
all its newsreaders were happy. They had been chosen originally for
their voices on radio rather than for their visual appeal and, while
some adapted to the new medium, others did not. There were new
techniques to be learned. One was to pace words to match the length
of film inserts and Lionel Marson, a slow reader, was sometimes seen
still relating one story after another piece of film had begun. Frank
Phillips and Alvar Liddell, two veteran radio newsreaders, made no
secret of their unhappiness on television. So, after a year of ITN, the

Robert Dougall was one of BBC's first television newsreaders

BBC picked three of its most personable readers, Richard Baker, Kenneth Kendall and Robert Dougall, as its answer to the ITN newscasters. They were to be seen and were even named.

In 1958 Hugh (later Sir Hugh) Greene, who had been a distinguished Fleet Street foreign correspondent and war reporter, became Director of News and Current Affairs and commissioned a report on television news from some of his younger executives. This proved to be highly critical of 'the emphasis placed on the arrival and departure of Cabinet Ministers, the inclusion of quotations from nondescript official or semi-official figures, the way in which platitudes and clichés uttered by an accepted public figure are so often presented to the viewer as significant statements'. It also found the manner of newscasters 'often soft and tentative'. Greene acted on the report and Stuart Hood, who took over as Editor of Television News in 1960, asked his staff to start thinking in terms of pictures rather than words. He also introduced newsreaders from the provinces and the dominions in an attempt to get away from the traditional BBC accent.

Gradually the two news organizations moved towards middle ground, the BBC becoming more human and ITN less brash. ITV spread across the country as the BBC had done earlier and the audiences for news grew. A milestone was the Cuba crisis of 1962 when America secured evidence of the establishment of Russian rocket bases on Cuba, ninety miles from the east coast of the United States. On the evening of Monday, 22 October, President John F. Kennedy appeared on US television with this warning: 'It shall be the policy of this nation to regard any nuclear missile launched from Cuba against any nation in the western hemisphere as an attack on the United States requiring a full retaliatory response upon the Soviet Union.' He announced that ships bound for Cuba would be stopped, searched and, if they contained weapons, turned back. US forces were on instant alert and the world was on the brink of atomic war. For a week the world waited, wondering if there was to be peace or annihilation. Newspapers were not immediate enough when devastation could be unleashed in minutes. Only radio and television could provide instant news and, with two television networks spanning the country, it was to television that the British public turned. On Sunday, 28 October, Khrushchev climbed down and gave orders for the rockets to be dismantled, crated and returned to the Soviet Union. The crisis was over. At the same time television was established as Britain's chief medium for news.

In 1957 a survey had shown that television was the main source of news for 24 per cent of the population, radio claiming 46 per cent and newspapers 30 per cent. By the end of 1962 television was the main

A year after ITN began the BBC picked newsreaders for television. Kenneth Kendall as he was then

source of news for 52 per cent and, while newspapers could claim 31 per cent, the proportion that relied on radio had shrunk to 17 per cent.

Chapter 2
News today

On all three channels the main news programme on weekdays now occupies a half-hour slot. The news expanded to this level in the second half of the sixties. America had shown the way: the CBS *Evening News with Walter Cronkite* had been introduced in September 1963 and was followed by NBC's *Huntley-Brinkley Report*. When BBC2 began in April 1964 it included a half-hour news programme, *Newsroom*. However, the audience for BBC2 was small – only ninety thousand homes in the early days – because the service was transmitted on the new UHF frequencies and viewers with VHF receivers were reluctant to buy new ones or have their old ones converted, particularly since BBC2 was widely reckoned to be a highbrow channel. BBC2 was the Cinderella channel, which it still remains.

Half-hour news first came to a major channel on 3 July 1967 when ITN introduced *News at Ten*. The ITN editor Sir Geoffrey Cox (he had been knighted the previous year) said at the time: 'At first sight it looks as if we are just lengthening the news, but that is not so. The revolutionary thing is that we are getting flexibility into it.' Until then news on television had always been given in short bulletins and in-depth coverage had been confined to current affairs programmes like the BBC's *Panorama* and ITV's *This Week*. These programmes were transmitted at fixed times on arbitrary days and were not related in any way to the flow of news. The first attempts at surmounting this problem were made by extending news programmes when big news broke. Extra time was allocated for war in the Middle East and when political party conferences were held. Then the news organizations began to screen special reports on momentous occasions such as President Kennedy's tour of Europe and the assassination of South Africa's premier, Hendrik F. Verwoerd. These developed into programmes like ITN's *Dateline*, the first regular late-night current affairs programme, but it was not mandatory for ITV companies to screen it, as it is for them to screen the news, and it was not shown in all regions. Therefore ITN could never withhold material from the news bulletins to show later in *Dateline* as the BBC was able to do when it established *Twenty-Four Hours*.

ITN decided that the answer was to combine news and news analysis in one programme which could either simply present the news in outline or present and interpret it simultaneously. For this a thirty-minute slot was needed, and to obtain it ITN had to put back its news to 10 pm. Earlier, in the heart of entertainment time, it would not be acceptable to the mass audience, declared the programme companies. Furthermore, it would split the evening into two halves and cause too many difficulties in scheduling – for example, ninety-minute dramas. From ITN's point of view 10 pm gave useful extra time for the preparation of the programme.

There was still nervousness in ITV about the programme before it began. Some executives feared that viewers would desert to the BBC, but Sir Geoffrey was confident that it would make good viewing. He pinned his faith on the growing amount of news available in television form because of the increase in Eurovision exchanges, satellite transmissions and the use of videotape. 'We are trying to prove,' he said, 'that the news of the day can fill half an hour either by its sheer dramatic quality or because it can be more readily assimilated if it has analysis at the time. News can hold an audience as a programme, a major part of everyone's viewing and not just a brief break into reality from the entertainment and escapism of TV.' On one night, he forecast, the programme might be filled by a single item such as a disaster or a war report. On another it might be possible to pack all the hard news into five minutes and allot the rest of the time to a major interview or a piece of film of human interest. There was to be no rigid pattern but, in general, viewers could expect more human interest stories and fuller coverage of sport.

ITN's studio presentation was changed for *News at Ten*. It adopted the American practice of using two newscasters – initially Alastair Burnet and Andrew Gardner. The reason was not simply a desire to offer visual variety; it had the practical advantage that, with news continuing to come in while the programme was on the air, fresh briefings could be given to whichever newscaster was out of shot.

The first two editions of *News at Ten* were received with some uncertainty both inside and outside ITN. On the third day ITN received from its reporter Alan Hart and a camera crew in Aden a vivid report on the Argyll and Sutherland Highlanders' retaking of the Crater district from rebels. 'It had action, tension, danger and a television natural in Colonel Mitchell,' recalls Sir Geoffrey. 'We ran it for eleven minutes – virtually the length of the old 9 pm bulletin – and it held the viewer for every second. When the viewing figures came in at the end of the week we knew we had the viewers with us.'

There was no doubt about it. By August 1969 ITN was getting all five editions of *News at Ten* into the weekly charts of the top twenty programmes. The BBC reshuffled its programmes to provide stiffer opposition and managed to break this pattern, then extended the news on BBC1 to half an hour, boldly slotting it at 9 pm. Later it also adopted the two-newscaster system, although it returned to using a

A television team films British Commandos searching vehicles in Aden

single reader in 1976. The *Nine O'Clock News* has also figured frequently in the top twenty. News, properly presented, is box office, as one television executive has put it.

News coverage on television has continued to increase. After the government lifted restrictions on the hours of broadcasting in 1972 ITN reintroduced a lunch-time news in *First Report*. Robert Kee was brought in to present it, not only newscasting but conducting interviews in the studio, over the telephone or by a television link, and even reading letters from viewers. In 1974 the BBC introduced ten minutes of news for children every afternoon from Monday to Thursday. Today both BBC1 and ITV carry three bulletins of national news every weekday. (Both also carry programmes of regional news, the subject of a later chapter.) BBC2 puts out two bulletins every weekday.

Current affairs programmes have developed alongside the news. The need for them is evident in a calculation Nigel Ryan, Editor of ITN, quoted in a letter to *The Times* in 1974: 'If a newscaster talked non-stop through a *News at Ten* programme,' he wrote, 'he could deliver almost 3,000 words; *The Times* prints about 130,000 words of news and sport daily.' In fact, because of its visual content, even a half-hour news bulletin carries fewer words than the front page of a broadsheet newspaper. But current affairs programmes have changed. In the early days both *Panorama* and *This Week* were magazines carrying a number of stories and in 1956 *This Week* used to pack up to half a dozen items into its half-hour. Today, because of the greater depth of news coverage, current affairs programmes tend to concentrate on just one story.

Organization

The BBC and ITN news and current affairs programmes look much alike today and their methods of working are similar, but the organization behind them is different. The BBC has a News and Current Affairs Division which services both radio and its two television channels. It is the largest organization of its kind in Europe and its editor is responsible directly to the Director-General. Since 1971 the editor has been Desmond Taylor, a Belfast man who was appointed at the age of forty-four after an early career on the *Northern Whig* and *Belfast Telegraph* before joining the BBC in 1954. His division is split into units and groups of units which are spread over three buildings in London alone. Radio News (which is not the concern of this book) is based at Broadcasting House, Television News at the Television Centre in Wood Lane, and Television Current Affairs at Lime Grove. Under Taylor, these have separate editors and staffs because of their different problems and concerns, such as television with visual coverage and radio with sound.

Television News acquired a new editor in 1976—Andrew Todd, a Scot who started as a journalist in Dundee but had been with BBC News in various capacities since the war. His department is responsible not only for the daily news programmes and the weekly BBC2 *News Review* for the deaf, but also for the weekly programmes *Westminster* and *Made in Britain*. However, *Panorama*, *Nationwide*, *Tonight*, *The Money Programme* and *Europa* are produced by current affairs units under Brian Wenham, once of ITN and subsequently Editor of *Panorama*.

ITN is owned jointly by ITV's fifteen programme companies. It is a non-profit-making company, relying upon the generosity of the companies for its money but, since *News at Ten* often reaches 14 million viewers, the companies obtain a high revenue from advertising before, during and after it. ITN has been based in Wells Street, just north of Oxford Street, since 1969, the year that BBC Television News moved from Alexandra Palace to the Television Centre. Its editor and chief executive, Nigel Ryan, read modern languages at Oxford before joining Reuters in 1954. He was a correspondent for the agency in Rome, Algeria, the Congo and South Africa before joining ITN, a move which came about through a meeting in the Congo with Robin Day, who was there representing *Panorama*.

ITN's business today is solely news. There was a time when it also made current affairs programmes, but it was obliged to drop its *Dateline* and *Reporting '67* to win the extra time to start *News at Ten* in 1967. Today all ITV's current affairs programmes come from the programme companies: *This Week* from Thames, *World in Action* from Granada and *Weekend World* from London Weekend Television. Of ITN's total staff of 460, some 100 are journalists, 270 are engineers and technicians and the remainder are administrative. Its overall budget is nearly £5 million a year. For its part BBC Television News has about 500 employees and can also call on the facilities and staff of radio news, though its budget is smaller.

On paper it is difficult to understand how such a small company as ITN, which means little to the public outside Britain and which maintains only one permanent staff foreign correspondent – in Washington – can compete with the might of the BBC, which is known throughout the world and maintains a corps of foreign correspondents. Because of its external radio services the BBC is widely regarded as the official voice of Britain. Yet ITN more than holds its own. Nigel Ryan admits that the BBC has greater resources but points out that ITN has a larger budget, which can buy resources. Other ITN executives claim that the BBC's size and reputation are counter-productive; because ITN is smaller it is leaner, can take decisions faster and deploy men more rapidly. And they suggest that the BBC's Establishment status is a handicap rather than a help: a foreign country with a grievance against Britain may impose sanctions against a BBC team while an ITN crew goes unhindered. This difference is marked by the attitudes within the two news organizations. At ITN they talk of a news programme as 'the show'. They are unashamedly dedicated to making programmes or 'shows' which, while informative and responsible, are yet as dramatic and entertaining as possible. They seek to blend journalism and show-business. At the BBC one feels the shadows of Lord Simon and Tahu Hole would fall across anyone irreverent enough to use a light-hearted term in relation to a news programme.

Chapter 3

Instant news

News has been defined as something of interest or importance that happened today. And the biggest advances in television news have been in showing today what happened today, sometimes as it happened, even when it happened in a far-off part of the world. In May 1937 it was accounted a marvel when BBC television showed live the coronation procession of King George VI. For it was the first major outside broadcast, the first time TV cameras (as opposed to film cameras) had been taken outside the grounds of Alexandra Palace, which housed the single studio. Television was in its infancy. It had begun as a regular service only six months earlier, the number of receivers was less than two thousand and they were confined to the area reached by the one transmitter at Alexandra Palace, which meant basically the London area. Cameras were not allowed inside Westminster Abbey, but three were installed on the processional route and an eight-mile cable linked a portable transmitter in a 4-ton lorry to Alexandra Palace. The primitive cameras, without turrets of inter-changeable lenses, much less zoom lenses, were on and below the plinth of Apsley Gate at Hyde Park Corner. One was positioned to show the approach of the procession, one to show it passing and the other to view its tail as it snaked towards Buckingham Palace.

The television crew had to be in their places by 4.30 am for the 2 pm broadcast and the morning was overcast and misty as they climbed to their places, soon to be besieged by crowds. As the morning passed the weather worsened and, ten minutes before the time for starting the transmission, rain began to fall, smudging the notes that commentator Freddie Grisewood had prepared in the margin of his programme. However, promptly at 2 pm the cameras began shooting and Grisewood began his commentary. The big moment came as the coach of the new king's mother, Queen Mary, approached Apsley Gate. She was bowing right and left and as she passed the cameras she inclined deliberately towards the lens. To viewers at home it seemed that she was acknowledging them personally.

The television crew failed to appreciate the gesture at the time; they were fearful that the poor light had ruined the programme. They did not know that at Alexandra Palace telephones were already ringing with calls from viewers reporting that they had seen the whole procession perfectly, apart from some mistiness which had not spoiled their enjoyment. Ten thousand had viewed the programme. 'We even had viewers ringing up from Ipswich and Brighton, which we had imagined lay outside our range,' wrote Grisewood in his autobiography.* 'So the whole thing had been a success after all, but never have I been so utterly exhausted. I reached home at 11 o'clock that night, fell into bed and slept for 24 hours without stirring. All of us, sound and television broadcasters alike, were literally out on our feet at the end of that memorable day.'

One by-product of that coronation broadcast was the development of a more sensitive Super Emitron camera tube.

Eurovision

By the time of the coronation of the present Queen on 2 June 1953 television was in a new age; it had spread throughout most of the more populated areas of Britain and could also reach Europe. Three years earlier, on 27 August 1950, the BBC had sent cameras to Calais to cover celebrations of the centenary of the completion of the submarine cable between Britain and France. There had been a two-hour programme from and about Calais, the world's first live television link between two countries. But it was not true international television; it could not be seen in France, the country of origin, because of the different line standards used.

* *The World Goes By* (London: Secker & Warburg 1952).

Richard Dimbleby in Calais for the first cross-Channel television programme in 1950

Richard Dimbleby and Sylvia Peters on the Eiffel Tower for a programme from Paris in 1952

A television picture is created by tracing out the scene before the cameras in a series of horizontal lines, subdivided into tiny elements. The light value of each element is scanned and transmitted in sequence from left to right and line by line to be rebuilt at the receiver in accordance with the transmitted signal, the process being fast enough to deceive the eye, which appears to see all the elements at once. The pictures from Calais were transmitted by British cameras on the British system of 405 lines, but France used 819 lines. (Other European countries used 625.)

However, in July 1952, Paris was linked live with London, and British and French viewers watched a programme simultaneously. This was achieved by training a camera operating on the British 405 line standard on the screen of a television set working on the French 819 line standard. It was a primitive method – today's equipment leaves the signal as a wave-form without being reconstituted as a picture during the conversion – and inevitably it resulted in a diminution of picture quality for British viewers, but it made possible the viewing by audiences in Europe of the coronation in 1953.

Early requests to televise the coronation ceremony had been refused, but Peter Dimmock, who was in charge of the BBC arrangements, had argued the case with a demonstration in Westminster Abbey, proving that the lighting required would not be excessive and

The Coronation – a royal coach passes a television camera point

White tie and tails was the dress for cameramen in the Abbey for the Coronation

that cameras need not be obtrusive, and eventually the decision was reversed although the actual crowning was not allowed to be screened.

The programme was to be television's longest broadcast up to that time – from 10 am, when Sylvia Peters, the studio announcer, introduced Berkeley Smith, the commentator outside Buckingham Palace, until 11.30 pm, when Richard Dimbleby, the commentator in the Abbey, said farewell. The day was a personal triumph for Dimbleby and a triumph also for television. A million new aerials had been erected in Britain for the occasion. An estimated 20 million Britons had crowded into public halls and the homes of friends to watch, compared with only 12 million who had listened on the radio. The television programme was also received in France, Germany, Holland and Belgium.

American viewers saw it too, but not live. NBC had originally drawn up a plan called Stratovision which required six aircraft circling at 40,000 feet and spaced 450 miles apart to relay the live coverage by microwave radio links. It was too ambitious. What actually happened was an air-race to be first to the United States with film. NBC and its rival CBS chartered aircraft and turned them into flying laboratories in which the film could be processed and commentaries added en route. But the NBC jet had to turn back and departure of the CBS one was delayed. Meanwhile an RAF bomber was on its way to Montreal with BBC film for the Canadian Broadcasting Corporation. America's ABC network, which had not made any special arrangements of its own, was able to beat NBC and CBS by several minutes by receiving and retransmitting the Canadian programme!

In Britain the coronation coverage changed attitudes to television. Its right to be present on major public occasions was established and the eminent came to accept it, if not to welcome it. The sale of sets soared, even though the *Radio Times* was still giving precedence to radio programmes. The programme also led to the forming of Eurovision – a name coined by George Campey, then a television journalist, now Head of BBC Publicity. The first major exchange of programmes between countries was in 1954. Another experiment took place in 1958 when five television services organized a daily 'hook-up' in sound and vision to exchange the best of the day's newsfilm. Pope Pius XII died and Pope John was elected to succeed him while the experiment was in progress, and viewers in Britain saw each night film shot earlier in the day in Rome. They saw the mourners in St Peter's Square, the assembly of the cardinals, the white smoke signal and the new pope in solemn procession.

The Eurovision links grew. In 1960 a broadcast by General de Gaulle was fed live from France into a BBC *Tonight* programme, and the Olympic Games in Rome were seen instantaneously by audiences

from Warsaw to the Pyrenees. In 1961 British viewers saw live coverage from Moscow of the fêting of Major Yuri Gagarin after the first
successful space flight. In return, the Russians received BBC pictures of
London's Trooping the Colour ceremony two months later. A daily
Eurovision exchange was established as a permanent arrangement.

Worldvision

Europe had become opened up to television by the land-lines and
microwave circuits of Eurovision. A similar organization called
Intervision linked the Iron Curtain countries. American networks
linked the United States and Canada. What was needed next was a
way of linking the continents to bring about worldvision.

The immediate target was to span the Atlantic with live television.
An early attempt was a system called Cablefilm, developed by BBC
engineers, which transmitted television pictures over the telephone
cable. Its first major use on a news occasion was for the Queen's visit
to Canada in 1959 to open the St Lawrence seaway, when viewers in
Britain were able to see the royal party's arrival in Newfoundland only
two hours earlier. 'BBC engineers, by exploiting the speed of light
itself, have come close to making television news as immediate as
radio,' boasted the BBC. But it was only practicable to use Cablefilm
for short flashes, because film had to be transmitted frame by frame
and sending one minute of film took a hundred minutes. Its last major
use was to transmit film of the assassination of President Kennedy in
Dallas in 1963. The BBC showed it in a special bulletin at 11 pm –
some four hours after the shooting.

But already Cablefilm was being superseded. Telstar, the first satellite capable of relaying television pictures across the world, had been
launched from Cape Canaveral in 1962. In eighteen minutes 200 million people in sixteen European countries saw baseball from Chicago,
a presidential press conference from Washington, the rocket-launching
site at Cape Canaveral, scenes from a performance of *Macbeth* in
Ontario, the World's Fair at Seattle, Niagara Falls and the United
Nations building in New York. On the satellite's next orbit pictures
from nine European capitals including London were transmitted to
North America, though the end of the programme was lost when
Telstar went out of range. It was only in line of sight from both sides
of the Atlantic for about eighteen minutes on each two-and-a-half-hour
orbit.

A year later came Early Bird, the first synchronous satellite on an
orbit such that it remained stationary 22,000 miles above the same
point on the earth's surface. The funeral of President Kennedy in 1963
was seen in Britain and twenty-two other countries as it happened,
relayed from Washington via the satellite. By 1968 viewers throughout

the world were able to see live pictures from the Mexico Olympics, and in 1969 Intelsat 3 (so named because it was put into space by the International Telecommunications Satellite Consortium) brought the first direct live exchanges with Japan.

The triumph of satellite communications came at 3.56 am (British time) on 21 July 1969 when 600 million people, a fifth of the world's population, saw American astronaut Neil Armstrong take man's first step on the moon at the climax of television's most extraordinary programme. Both BBC and ITN had to rely on the same pictures supplied from mission control at Houston, Texas. The competition as to how best they could be presented and interpreted was, according to an overwhelming vote of the critics, won by ITV's programme *Man on the Moon.*

ITV's show began at 6 pm on Sunday, 20 July and blended news and entertainment in a new way. David Frost hosted the entertain-

Cameras and a giant television screen in Trafalgar Square for ITV's programme on the night of the moon landing

ment part of the show from London Weekend Television's studios, which were then at Wembley. He opened with these words: 'Hello and good evening to the night of the great adventure, the night of drama ... the end of an incredible voyage and the beginning of what may be a whole new world for all of us. Because tonight man lands on the moon and steps into the age of Flash Gordon and Dan Dare.' The programme then switched to the simulated moon craters at the ITN studio (then in Kingsway) and to Alastair Burnet presiding over a two-man panel comprised of Peter Fairley, the ITN science correspondent, and Paul Haney, the former 'voice of Apollo', who had been heard speaking from Houston in an official capacity during previous Apollo missions. For twelve hours their explanations of what was going on in space, with typed caption flashes superimposed to report developments, were interspersed with satellited pictures from Houston, and Frost's incongruous guests who included Cilla Black and

Man on the moon – descending the steps of the lunar module

Engelbert Humperdinck singing, and Lord Hailsham and Dame Sybil Thorndike answering phone-in questions from viewers. The BBC had decided to continue normal programmes until nearer the time of the landing.

ITV's programme ran for more than nine hours before the pictures were shown that the world had been awaiting – Neil Armstrong stepping on to the moon's surface. At this point producer David Nicholas, Deputy Editor of ITN, left the words to the astronauts themselves, and viewers listened to Armstrong speaking from outside the lunar module (LEM): 'I'm at the foot of the ladder. And I step off the LEM now. That's one small step for man; one giant leap for mankind.'

When ITV closed down at 6.22 am on Monday it had completed its longest continuous broadcast. It had been a television occasion, signified by the fact that whereas hitherto explorers had planted a flag to mark a new conquest, the astronauts were in addition to leave behind a television camera. Television had claimed the event for all mankind.

The BBC's audience research figures for four o'clock that morning, the time of the moonwalk, calculated that 3.5 million were watching ITV and 2.5 million BBC1. It was the first time the BBC admitted to defeat by ITV on a major occasion.

Today satellites cover the world, relaying television pictures between a network of earth stations. Film that once took a day to reach London even by jet aircraft can now be transmitted in minutes once it reaches a so-called electronic area. And live transmissions can be seen all over the world as they happen. The cost is high, but when the news is important or dramatic the public now expect it instantly.

Chapter 4
Gathering the news

The heart of a news organization is its editorial floor. At the BBC Television Centre it is the sixth floor. At ITN headquarters in Wells Street it is the first floor, and in the centre of the big room are six desks, three concerned with what is known as input and three with output. Input – called intake at the BBC – means gathering the news and getting the stories into the office; output means selecting, processing and packaging this material for the screen. The input desks consist of the news desk, the foreign desk and the assignments desk. The news desk briefs and despatches reporters on home stories. The foreign desk handles all news from abroad, whether it is being covered by ITN staff or by other organizations. The assignments desk, working in close liaison, controls the camera crews. These three desks service all three of ITN's daily programmes though, since *News at Ten* is more than twice as long as the 5.30 pm bulletin, the same stories may be treated at very different length. The output desks are concerned with the production respectively of the lunch-time bulletin, the early evening programme known at ITN as 'the early' and *News at Ten*, which is known as 'the late'. Each desk is presided over by a producer, who is responsible for the content of that particular programme.

Part of the ITN news room – on the right the News at Ten *desk*

Between these desks sit production assistants and typists with a range of duties from typing copy to timing bulletins. In one corner is the tape-room, in which teleprinters chatter out stories from British and foreign news agencies, the same messages that are going into Fleet Street newspaper offices and that provide the basic raw material of most news operations. They supply some 400,000 words a day, which is about 130 times as many as the longest bulletin can use. (The BBC also has its unique monitoring service, which listens to foreign broadcasting stations around the clock.) Another wire machine receives photographs transmitted by the picture agencies. Along one wall is a row of five cutting-rooms, accessible to anyone needing to see film as it is being edited. Against the opposite wall are the desks of scriptwriters and reporters and a room for the specialist correspondents who cover political, diplomatic, industrial, economic and science stories. Against another wall are the offices of the deputy editor and the two assistant editors who are responsible for the day-to-day news handling. Other vital parts of the television news machine are located on other floors above and below, but it is in this room that the main action is centred.

The start of the day

The news editor of the day arrives on the editorial floor at about 8 am to start a shift that will continue until *News at Ten* has been transmitted that night. To preserve continuity, key executives work long shifts, compensated for by working only a certain number of days every month. So, unlike a newspaper, television news has more than one news editor, foreign editor and chief sub-editor.

The news editor will already have digested the contents of the morning newspapers and listened to the latest news on radio; his first task is to begin updating the schedule for the day that he or his predecessor prepared the day before. A number of reporters and film crews will be in the field already, covering, or preparing to cover, stories for the day's programmes. For the majority of stories are predictable to some extent. Court cases, demonstrations, conferences and parliamentary debates will be known in advance, though their outcome may be uncertain. Bombings, accidents, murders and other unforeseeable occurrences are in the minority. The news editor talks on the telephone to his Manchester-based staff reporter who covers the North, his opposite numbers in the regional ITV companies to see what news stories they have in prospect, sifts tapes from the agencies and takes calls from freelance correspondents and informants.

At the foreign desk the foreign editor is performing a similar task, assessing what may be expected from ITN staff abroad and from UPITN, an agency part-owned by ITN which, apart from distributing ITN material abroad, maintains its own staff in a number of capitals.

He is also in contact with other television stations in the Eurovision network through the European Broadcasting Union, which has administrative headquarters in Geneva and its technical centre in Brussels.

Every day the member organizations, representing twenty-three major countries, exchange their major items of news in a bring-and-buy sale. The process begins with a morning link-up, chaired in rotation for periods of a fortnight by the different foreign editors. The main language is English, though French is also used. Each country declares what it expects to be able to offer during the day. ITN will announce its intended offerings and so will the BBC and the French, German, Italian and other networks. At ITN a secretary makes a shorthand note of all the stories on offer, including the length of the running-time of the film, perhaps one minute ten seconds or one minute fifty-four seconds, and whether it will carry sound or be mute.

At 10.30 am news editor, foreign editor and assignments editor join other executives in the editor's office for the morning conference. They make their reports on the stories in prospect, from a kidnapping abroad to a film star's wedding at home. The respective merits are discussed and the editor rules on matters of policy. The conference lasts about twenty minutes and then they return to their desks. The foreign editor sends a Telex message to Geneva, accepting or rejecting the foreign stories on offer through the Eurovision exchange. The news editor and assignments editor have reporters and crews to brief.

Reporting teams

The front-line troops of the news organization are the reporters and film crews, which consist of a cameraman and a sound recordist, supplemented by a lighting engineer in case the shooting has to be indoors or in poor light conditions. ITN has sixteen of these crews. Cameraman and sound recordist travel in a car with radio telephone in which their equipment is always ready for use. One or other will take the car home at night so that they can get away quickly on an assignment at any time. The reporter and lighting engineer will generally travel in separate cars, for all or any may have to move independently to other assignments.

The decision to commit a reporter and crew is not taken lightly. More complex considerations are involved than in a newspaper sending out a reporter, who can work alone and telephone his copy from any call-box. Time is the great problem. A story breaks perhaps sixty miles from London. It may take two hours to get there, two hours to do the job, two hours to get back. Allowing forty-five minutes each for processing the film, editing it and dubbing a commentary, makes a total of more than eight hours, which may barely leave time to catch

Destruction on Dawson's Field

A CID chief faces a reporter, sound recordist and cameraman from ATV Today

the main programme. A despatch rider on a motorcycle – one of a dozen maintained by ITN – might be able to cut the time by meeting the crew at an arranged place and rushing the film back to ITN. Alternatively, the crew could save time by putting the film on a train, or it might be possible for them to move on from the story to the headquarters of a regional ITV company and inject it into ITN 'down the line' from there. Again, it may be better to leave the story to the regional company to cover, or to employ a 'stringer', a local freelance cameramen. But ITN prefers to use its own crews whenever possible because they know the organization's policy and the amount of film footage likely to be used.

The word television newsmen use to cover these considerations of manpower deployment is 'logistics' and it is impossible to discuss television news coverage for long without hearing the term. Much money is expended on getting material back quickly. When the Prime Minister made an urgent visit to the Queen at Balmoral, film crews went there and a helicopter was chartered to fly their film from Balmoral to Glasgow. There it was processed, cut by an editor sent up from ITN, and piped down the line to Wells Street from the Scottish Television studios. The arrangements were worked out by the assignments desk.

When a film team is abroad – and two or three may be at any given time – the arrangements are likely to be even more complex. Once it was a race to get film on to the first available aircraft to London. There is still a race to get film on aircraft, but no longer does the aircraft have to be bound for England. The race is to get the film to a point from which it can be transmitted by satellite. During the war in Cyprus film was flown to Tel Aviv for processing and editing, then satellited from Israel to Italy where it was fed into the Eurovision network. On major stories the news organizations now send out back-up teams of technicians, sometimes headed by a producer, to cut the time involved. This system came into being when three airliners were skyjacked to Dawson's Field in Jordan in 1970. With two crews in the field for the first time, ITN felt that a producer should go out to mastermind coverage on the spot. In this instance the producer, David Phillips, had no sooner set foot on Jordanian soil than the three aircraft were blown up, but he acquired the only close-up film of the £10 million blaze. The authorities would not let any scheduled airliners out of Amman airport that night because of the risk of sabotage, so, with a journalist from America's CBS, he chartered a Caravelle jet from the Jordanian airline which flew them to Nicosia with the film. On that occasion it was quicker to fly the film on to London than to try to inject it from a satellite area, but it was then satellited around the world from London and won a newsfilm award.

ITN had now moved into the world's big league in its coverage of foreign stories. When the Arab–Israeli war broke out in 1973 it sent twenty people, but competition was fierce. ITN had three crews in the field, America's ABC had eight and CBS nine. And because Tel Aviv had only one film processing laboratory the Americans flew in their own portable one. This is likely to become standard practice, because an organization can still offset a large part of its heavy costs if it is the first one to make its film available for world-wide distribution.

An alternative to a film crew is to use electronic television cameras and a mobile outside broadcast unit. ITN owns one of the most compact OB units in the country, housed on a Range Rover chassis with an extended wheelbase. It includes three hand-held video cameras and a video tape recorder, sound and vision mixing equipment and microwave link facilities. The unit can transmit pictures live or record them on videotape and they can be played into a news programme without processing. But for live transmissions it is necessary to set up a radio link to send the signals back to the studio. The team have to erect a transmitting aerial on a high point such as a roof, close to the scene. A very high frequency signal is focused by a dish on the aerial like the beam from a torch. It is received by another mast, aligned with the transmitting aerial. It is possible to beam the signal fifty miles or more blind over clear country, but over long distances, or where there are hills in the way, the signal may have to be passed from one aerial to another. The TV camera and OB unit are ideal when there

ITN's outside broadcast unit

is no time to spare, such as reporting from outside the House of Commons on a division taking place while *News at Ten* is on the air. The television camera is more sensitive than a film camera and can work in lower light levels. It is cheaper to operate, in that no colour film stock is required and videotape is reusable. But it requires a bigger crew; the OB unit is not yet as mobile or as self-contained as a film crew. One day television cameras will be much more widely used, replacing film cameras as the main tools of the television newsmen, but that day has not yet arrived.

Film exchange and videotaping
At midday comes the first Eurovision exchange, known as EVN Zero. This curious designation is because there used to be a main exchange

at 5 pm and an additional exchange of late news at 7.30 pm, known respectively as EVN 1 and EVN 2. They continue, but the noon exchange has subsequently been introduced and has consequently been designated EVN Zero.

In Wells Street the Eurovision identification card comes up on the monitors. Then the film stories available are run, each of them preceded by a card showing the origin, from RAI (Italy), ORTF (France), TVE (Spain), ARD (Hamburg), or wherever. There is only a brief gap between each piece of film. In addition to the fixed time exchanges there may be a 'hot-line' link-up if a big story, such as an assassination, breaks, and the story will be flashed around Europe in seconds. Every organization takes out a story from time to time, but they also put them in. There is no fee for the stories, the costs of the operation being divided between the participating countries on a sliding scale according to the estimated number of TV sets in each country, so that Britain, for example, pays considerably more than Ireland. The stories required are videotaped as they are received, and the quality of videotaped pictures is now high.

The first ventures in recording programmes were made by pointing a film camera at the screen of a high quality monitor set. This system, called Telerecording, was used to record the coronation in 1953, but it involved loss of quality and was expensive and there was no way of knowing the result until the film had been processed. Attention turned to magnetic tape as used in sound recording. The main problem was the high speed at which the tape needed to run in order to accommodate the wider range of frequencies of video signals compared with audio signals. Early experiments involved a speed of 250 inches per second, which was not practical. The breakthrough came from the United States, where there was an additional need for recording because of the time differences between the coasts. The Ampex videotape recorder first shown there in 1956 solved the problem by means of revolving recording heads and transverse scanning – using the tape across its width rather than its length. Four recording heads on a drum rotated at 250 revolutions per minute to scan across the centre of a 2-inch wide tape moving along at 15 inches per second. One edge of the tape was used for the sound-track and the other for a control track. There were still problems in editing tape. Cutting and splicing it like film was dangerously imprecise and so editing was avoided as far as possible. However, as the quality of videotape recording improved it became possible to edit by re-recording from the original tape to a second tape, merely stopping and restarting the tapes as required for deletions, insertions or transpositions.

Now editing is done electronically. By the time it has begun the tempo on the first floor in Wells Street has increased considerably. By afternoon the despatch riders are roaring back with film packages for the processing labs. At 4.30 pm the executives hold another conference, generally known as 'the look-ahead' because its main purpose is to look ahead to the next day's activities. Not that the news gathering day is over. The collection of news is a continuous, round-the-clock process, and it is worth considering the operations of reporters and film crews in greater detail before proceeding to the way in which material is selected and prepared for transmission.

Chapter 5

Reporters

The reporter is the leader of the three-man television news film team. Not its boss in the normal sense, for the three work as a team and all contribute ideas and initiative. No reporter would try to give orders to the cameraman about filming, since that is the cameraman's job and, as television is a visual medium, pictures are more valuable than words and the cameraman is in some ways the most important member of the team. However, in deciding where to go, when to start, whom to interview and how long to allow, the reporter makes the decisions. It is the reporter who talks the team's way into places and situations, and fixes the interviews – and he may well spend longer on telephones than in putting anything on film. It is the reporter, too, who gets most of the kudos, for he is always identified by name in a programme. The cameraman rarely is and the recordist virtually never. The reporter gets the 'herograms', the messages of congratulation on a job well done, but on the other hand he is the one who takes the blame if the team falls down on a job.

Reporters who come into television, often in the regions, do so from a variety of backgrounds. The BBC's Peter Stewart was for many

Reporter Trevor MacDonald

years a Fleet Street reporter whose presence on a story invariably caused concern to rivals. Trevor MacDonald, ITN's West Indian reporter, was formerly a BBC radio reporter. Michael Nicholson, one of TV's most travelled foreign correspondents, had little experience of journalism apart from editing a university paper and working in the London office of the Scottish *Sunday Post* before joining ITN. He was one of a number of ITN reporters, including Gerald Seymour, Peter Sissons, Peter Snow and Richard Wakely, who were taken on by ITN as graduate trainees and then, after screen-tests involving reading scripts and conducting mock interviews, spent six months in the office learning something about sub-editing and writing stories for newscasters before being sent out on the road with an experienced camera crew. In the beginning, reporters learn from cameramen. Michael Nicholson recalls:

'My very first story was at Wandsworth where a couple of men who had been arrested by Scotland Yard were in hospital being treated. A couple of their buddies turned up one morning and released them and I did a stand-upper outside the hospital. I had one of our top cameramen with me, Len Dudley, now dead, and he directed me. He said, "Go and write your piece, it's got to be forty-five seconds long." I said, "I can't do it in forty-five seconds," and he said, "If you don't do it in forty-five seconds they won't use it." I said, "Well how will I know it's forty-five seconds?" and he said, "Jesus Christ! Three words per second."

'So I wrote my piece sitting in the car, and timed it roughly and he said, "Right, stand there, start talking and when you see my hand go up, start walking to that spot by the door." I said, "Talk and walk at the same time! I can't do that." He said, "Well, we'll rehearse it a few times." So I did three or four dry runs and he said, "Now let's try a take." And we did two or three takes and it went on the screen that night.

'It was one of the first bits of direction I had, and a very important little bit of direction too, because you don't walk unless there is a reason for it. You can't just stroll up a road or people will ask, "Where's he going?" You only walk if there is a reason, and if you can find a reason it looks good. In this case I walked from the point where the two crooks entered the hospital to the front door where they and the men they rescued got out.'

Every reporter gets early instruction like this from a cameraman, and the cameraman continues to act as director until the reporter has graduated in the eyes of the crew. It is important that he has the trust of the crew because, if the team is to move fast when it has to, the reporter must be able to call his colleagues at 2 am and say, 'Quick! Get some clothes on and meet me downstairs in ten minutes,' and get instant compliance, explaining later why and where they are going.

The 'stand-upper' is one of the basic skills of the TV reporter. It is a short piece delivered into camera. Sometimes it is delivered by the reporter simply to show that he is not in a studio but on the spot where the action is happening or has happened. Sometimes he appears before the camera to connect two different angles of a story, to change the situation from one spot to another. When he begins 'Twenty minutes ago on this spot . . .' he is disguising failure, in that television was not there when the event took place, but of course television cannot always reach the scene while the action is happening.

Outside the studio, away from teleprompters, the reporter will have to memorize his words, though few find any difficulty in this because the into-camera piece is short, possibly only thirty seconds. Viewers become bored at being addressed directly for long. Two and a half minutes is a long piece into-camera and will probably be done in a studio. The experienced reporter does not always even write out his words in advance, but he must be able to deliver them without hesitation. Viewers will accept hesitation and gestures while searching for the right word when they know that the reporter is making a live outside broadcast and speaking off the cuff, but on film he is expected to be word perfect and so, if he fluffs a line, he will have to record it again. Reading from notes is regarded as unacceptable under normal circumstances, suggesting as it does that the reporter cannot remember what happened. The exceptions are when he is quoting figures or an excerpt from a speech, which conveys precision and a sense of authenticity. He may also use a notebook when reporting a court case, particularly as on a major trial he may have to do two hasty stand-uppers a day – a concise story for the early bulletin and a longer one for the late. Moreover, there are dire legal perils for a slip of the tongue.

One gimmick employed when the story involves names that are difficult to pronounce, frequently the case in a country like Africa, is for the reporter to write the names phonetically on his hand or when practicable chalk them on the ground in front of him. He can glance down and make it seem like a natural pause.

Interviewing

Another basic skill required of a reporter is interviewing, though the news reporter probably makes less use of interviews than the reporter for current affairs programmes. Interviewing for television is a vastly different matter to interviewing for a newspaper. The newspaperman, intentionally or accidentally, develops a technique. He may affect a diffident manner, suggesting a harmless, ingenuous approach. He can dissemble about the real purpose of the interview, giving the impression that he is ridding himself of a rather boring chore. He can ask innocuous questions until, having lured his interviewee into a false sense of security, he casually drops in an incisive one. Finally, he can present to the public a highly selective version of the conversation. A television reporter cannot do this; he will be seen in action. He has perhaps two and a half minutes of screen-time, during which he must put the questions as succinctly as possible and in a form requiring more than a 'yes' or 'no' answer. In fact, there is one necessary piece of deception in a television interview as screened. Since the camera cannot focus closely on both interviewer and subject at once, the questions are normally repeated and filmed after the interview. This also provides 'cut-away' shots, so that the interview may be abbreviated, with the cuts bridged by shots of the reporter asking questions or listening to the subject. However, the subject is invited to remain until the cut-aways are filmed, and the reporter endeavours to repeat his questions in exactly the same words.

Interviewing has changed radically since the early days of television. In the days before ITN, the reporter approached a VIP with a respectful, 'Have you had a good trip, sir? Would you be kind enough to say something, sir? Can you tell us anything about the progress of your talks, sir?' The historic interview which highlighted the change was carried out by Robin Day for ITN in June 1957, six months after the Suez crisis. Day interviewed President Nasser of Egypt in the garden of his Cairo home. The countries involved were not even talking officially; indeed, Britain was still technically at war with Egypt. But Nasser told Day to 'ask anything you like'. Day asked, 'Is it right that you now accept the permanent existence of Israel as an independent sovereign state?' Nasser replied, 'Well, you know, you are jumping to conclusions.' Day retorted with the touch of asperity that has since become familiar, 'No, I am asking a question.'

This style of interviewing caused shock-waves. The television critic Denis Thomas wrote of Day at this period: 'He puts his blunt, loaded questions with the air of a prosecuting counsel at a murder trial. As he swings back to face the cameras, metaphorically blowing on his knuckles, one detects the muffled disturbance as his shaken victim is led away.' Yet Day was and is scrupulously fair. Unfortunately he was copied by reporters with less ability and there were instances of rudeness rather than firmness, a desire to dominate rather than establish facts. But it rapidly became apparent that to push too hard was counter-productive; the viewer's sympathies swung from the reporter to the subject and the phase has generally passed.

Resistance to television interviewing has also largely gone. Most statesmen and politicians probably prefer an interview by television

Robin Day making history by his interview with President Nasser

ITN reporter Anthony Carthew interviews James Callaghan

because they know that if they are filmed talking they cannot be misquoted. They may, and probably will, be cut, but the words that remain will be their own. And an interview on television will often be transcribed by newspapers, whereas one given to a paper is often exclusive and will therefore be ignored by rivals. It is not usual to tell interviewees in advance the questions they will be asked, as the result tends to look glib and rehearsed. Normally the subject is merely fore-warned of the area that it is hoped to cover.

The commentary

While a personality reporter such as Alan Whicker is permitted some latitude in presenting a personal view in current affairs programmes, the news reporter is theoretically permitted none. He must not editor-ialize. It is often difficult to avoid this; a question worded without sufficient thought may convey an implication which was not intended. But television is not as slavish now as it was. Michael Nicholson says:

'If I'm interviewing a terrorist who has just blown up a VC10 with 150 people on board I am not going to appear to try to understand him. I'm going to thump him as hard as I can. But if it is an interview with somebody like Ian Smith, the Prime Minister of Rhodesia, how many people in this country sympathize with him? A lot, I would think, so you cannot knock him hard. I think it is fairly easy to make your mind up when you should be sympathetic and where you should be knocking and where no sort of bias should be allowed to show at all.

'Years ago in Vietnam, on a cease-fire assignment, I did a story, and two days later I went back to the same village and it had been flat-tened. Two days into the cease-fire and there were babies all over the place and bodies and little kitchen utensils. I could not help it, I thought, for twenty-five years these people have been waiting for a cease-fire and this is it, and I did what for me was a very emotional piece to camera and there was much reaction this end. Some people thought I had been out there too long and should be brought back because I was tired. Other people were saying, "It really got me". I don't see how you can be objective in a situation like that. How can you be objective when a quarter of a million people have died in an earthquake or a flood and say, "But next year it may not rain"?'

Ideally the commentary should be recorded under studio condi-tions, without echoes and without noises like car horns or aircraft engines. Away from a studio, quiet countryside is usually better than indoors, but in a city both can be impossible. Even a throat micro-phone may pick up sounds of an hotel's air-conditioning plant, so the sound recordist will often erect a primitive shelter of mattresses and bedding in his hotel bedroom, into which the reporter crawls with a torch to read his commentary. This is not always possible. During the civil war in Amman, Michael Nicholson recorded a commentary in a lavatory at Beirut airport, stopping every few minutes as an aircraft took off or a chain was pulled and a toilet flushed!

With all the constituent parts of a report completed, the reporter faces the problem of getting it back to the studio or to a regional studio from which it can be piped down the line, or, if abroad, delivering it to an airport or satellite station. While the crew are unloading the film and packing it into tins inside a changing bag, the reporter transfers the notes of his story to a 'treatment' for the benefit of the film editor and others at headquarters. Down the right-hand half of the page he writes or types the story, and on the left-hand side he lists the shots that illustrate it. For example, on the right: 'John Smith lives in fear, surrounded by a barbed-wire fence, an early warning system and powerful lights.' On the left: 'Roll one, Smith walking towards barbed-wire fence. Roll two, dogs running from barn. Shots of lights in trees.'

Then the reporter writes a 'dope sheet'. Strictly speaking, this is the cameraman's job, but it is often done by the reporter while the cameraman is cleaning and reloading his camera. It gives a detailed list of all the shots by roll numbers. When the film editor looks at this, he can see that the shot of the dogs running from the barn is half-way through roll two. Since a roll of film is 400 feet long he can run quickly through 200 feet to locate the shot.

Abroad, unless there is a trusted shipper, the reporter will escort the film package to the airport to make sure it gets on a plane. If possible, he will find a 'pigeon', a friendly passenger to take charge of it and hand it over to the news organization's representative on arrival. Otherwise he will have to complete customs and air-freight documents and deal with other formalities. A pigeon is preferred – though on one occasion, when a plane from Saigon arrived unexpectedly early in Hong Kong, ITN had to track down pigeon and film in a bar. Yet even when the film has been despatched the reporter is not necessarily finished with the job. It has become common practice to update a film package with a live report by telephone during the bulletin.

Logistics

Television reporters need the same qualities as all reporters: a desire to discover the truth, the knowledge and skill to get the facts, and an ability to present them in a way that is easy to follow. The television reporter also needs a high degree of knowledge of television logistics. Some television reporters claim that 90 per cent of their work is concerned with getting into a position to report and getting the material back.

The first problem is getting to the scene. After the 1974 coup in Cyprus all the news media were trying to get to the island, but inevitably all flights had been discontinued. Both the BBC and ITN had teams in Athens, Ankara and Beirut waiting to get to Cyprus. ITN also had a team in Tel Aviv, but the BBC did not, and the first plane into Cyprus after the coup was one from Tel Aviv and it carried Michael Nicholson, who was thus able to get the first interview with the new president, Nicos Sampson.

The clock is the constant enemy. In Israel during the war with Egypt it could take six hours to get to the front line. But, having spent four hours there, the reporter had to call it a day, however much or little he had obtained, and race to get his report back to Tel Aviv by 3 pm because processing might take until 4 pm and editing until 6 pm, and this was near the deadline for getting it on the satellite.

There are often problems in leaving the scene of action with a story. After an avalanche engulfed the village of Val-d'Isère in France in 1970, Keith Hatfield got in but police refused to let anyone leave because of the danger of further avalanches. Hatfield hitched his way out on a snow-clearing bulldozer, hiding behind the driver's seat. After two miles he picked up another lift in a milk-truck. After another seven miles along slippery mountain roads he reached a village where he was able to hire a taxi to Geneva. There he was able to catch a plane to London with his report.

Support from the foreign desk in London is important in these circumstances. ITN reporters speak highly of the back-up provided for them by the foreign desk. By the time they reach Heathrow on their way to an assignment there will normally be waiting for them a large envelope containing relevant newspaper cuttings, a map and the names and addresses of contacts who may help them. ITN's foreign desk is also praised for its messages to reporters in the field, which go beyond the 'herograms' which it is customary to send to reporters who have done a good job. The foreign desk knows that a major concern of the man at work thousands of miles away is how his material has been received. A typical cable to a reporter reads: INTERVIEW AIRED AT 4 MINUTES 50. THANKS, LED SECOND HALF. ASK MARIO TO CHECK SOUND GEAR AS SOF HAD NO BASS AND SOUNDED TINNY. REGARDS THANKS AND APOLOGIES NOT LONGER. This tells the reporter that his interview was given four minutes fifty seconds on the screen and was used to open the second half of *News at Ten*. It also instructs him to tell the cameraman that the SOF (sound on film) quality was disappointing.

This interview had been a scoop but, if the BBC had been present, the cable would also have told the reporter what sort of coverage the rival service had given the story. If the story had not been used the reporter would have been given the reasons.

Television reporters are inevitably much travelled and experienced in all aspects of life and death. They may be in the luxury of an international hotel at one moment and under fire a few hours later – or even at the same time. Keith Hatfield recalls the skyjacking of airliners to the Jordan desert in 1970:

'When I arrived, the Jordan war had not yet started. I was shown up to a pleasant room in the Intercontinental Hotel in Amman and all was very normal. But a few days later I had my bed turned on its side against the window to keep out flying bullets. I was sleeping on the corridor floor. Dinner had become a matter of a bowl of rice. The going rate for a bottle of beer was £2 and you could pay as much as £5 and a packet of cigarettes for a roll of lavatory paper. But when I came to leave I was presented with a full bed-and-board bill to pay. And the final blow was that a $12\frac{1}{2}$ per cent service charge had been added!'

Problems are not confined to assignments abroad. When ITN was located at Television House in Kingsway, which also housed the Rediffusion programme company, one of its reporters, Tom St John Barry, struggled for twenty minutes with shrieking teenagers to get into the building with film of an interview with R. A. Butler at London Airport. These teenagers were besieging Television House in their efforts to get auditions for the pop programme *Ready, Steady, Go!*

John Edwards, an ITN reporter who subsequently became head of current affairs at Thames Television, waited outside 10 Downing Street for Sir Alec Douglas-Home on the day he became premier. Sir Alec was supposed to be there at 2.15 pm but did not arrive until 2.35 pm. Edwards was on screen live from 2.10 onwards and had to ad-lib for twenty-five minutes. 'I even went into the details of his innings at Lords for Eton on a tricky wicket against Harrow,' he recalls.

In an age of increased specialization, in journalism as in everything else, the number of specialist reporters has been growing over the years. As on a newspaper, the specialists like the diplomatic correspondent and the science reporter are expected to discover and bring in their own stories as well as being available to provide quick, expert interpretation of stories that break without warning. At one time women reporters were in the specialist category, being mainly used to cover fashions and other 'feminine' subjects, but reporters like Jacky Gillott broke down barriers by insisting on being allowed to cover any story, apart possibly from war (where the objections are from the military rather than from the girls).

Chapter 6

Film crews

Reporters and film crews have to work as a team or their job is impossible. In action, for instance, in a London street or on a foreign battleground, reporter, cameraman and sound recordist are linked by cable – or at least their equipment is. The lead from the reporter's microphone connects with the sound man's amplifier, while another lead connects the amplifier, hung from the sound man's neck, to the camera, carried at the operator's shoulder. They must watch each other closely because if, say, the cameraman, peering into his view-finder, starts to run, the others must run too. If the sound recordist is intent on his meters and slow off the mark the cameraman will be brought back with a jerk, and if the reporter is not wary he may bump the cameraman. (Although crews have radio microphones which do not require physical connection, they are not greatly used, because sometimes there is sound interference and, in addition, they involve the use of a bulky box which cannot be carried easily.)

Equipment

A reporter may work with a number of different crews, but the camera-man and sound engineer normally constitute a permanent partner-ship. Unlike the reporter, whose heaviest piece of equipment is likely to be a portable typewriter, they travel with a daunting amount of hardware. The chief and most expensive item among it is a sound camera, costing about £7,000. News film is invariably shot with com-bined sound by what is known as the single system. (Documentary films are commonly shot by the double system, with the sound on a tape recorder linked to the camera by electrical synchronization, and later transferred to another roll of film. This gives better quality results and greater flexibility, but for the news the sound does not need to be up to hi-fi standard.)

In the early days of television news, sound was recorded on film optically, an image being created on the film by a hairline light from a galvanometer responsive to audio modulations. Today magnetic 'stripe' is used. The sound-track is in the form of a strip of ferrous oxide along one edge of the film. After the film has passed through the picture gate it travels on to the sound recording head, which creates magnetic patterns on the stripe. In effect, the camera embodies a miniature tape recorder. One complication about this system is that twenty-eight frames must run through the picture gate before the film reaches the sound-head. This means that the sound is never alongside the picture to which it relates but twenty-eight frames ahead, posing some difficulties in the cutting-room. A revolution came about in news photography when the BBC began to use 16-mm film cameras in place of the bulky 35-mm cameras of the documentary film-makers and newsreel cameramen. The Korean war had proved these to be too unwieldy. Experiments followed with 8, 9.5, 16 and 17.5-mm formats before 16 mm was selected as giving the best quality. The camera that was chosen was the Auricon Cine Voice. It had been designed for amateur use and was only equipped to hold 100 feet of film which is shot in less than three minutes. This was not adequate, so the BBC converted the camera to take a 400 feet magazine (giving just over ten and a half minutes) and this has become the standard loading though, since there is always some wastage at the beginning and end of a film, there may be only five or six usable minutes on a roll. ITN was equipped from the beginning with the Auricon and, twenty years later, some of the original cameras are still in regular use, though it also has the latest models which are much lighter.

There have been proposals that a switch might be made to the 8-mm Super 8 format introduced for amateur use by Kodak in 1965. It has been used by television crews, usually for clandestine filming in countries where uncensored news is unpopular. A typical example was when *This Week* decided to go into Czechoslovakia in 1973 to film life there five years after the Russians had crushed Alexander Dubček's liberalizing regime. Because he knew that television would either be refused permission to enter the country or, if granted permission, would be restricted and censored, John Edwards, the producer at that time, sent a reporter and his girl friend, who had not the damning description 'Journalist' in their passports, to pose as tourists with amateur cine cameras. The cameras are cheap, costing only hundreds as against thousands for 16 mm and they are light to use. But they pose problems. It is not easy to fit 8-mm film into a system geared to handling 16 mm, and it is difficult to examine the small images on the film with the unaided eye. Editing also is more difficult. Most cameramen feel that the next big change will be to the video camera.

Development never ceases. In the early days cameras were equipped with 'turrets', revolving plates mounting three lenses of different focal lengths – a wide angle, a standard lens and a telephoto – and the cameraman switched from one to another by swivelling the turret. Today a single zoom lens is fitted, which gives continuous adjustment from wide to telephoto angles of acceptance. The standard zoom lens is a 10 to 1, equal to focal lengths of from 12 to 120 mm. For cricket, a distant shot of a rocket launching and other assignments where a longer lens is required, the cameraman can switch to a 20 to 1 zoom, but these are needed only rarely and require the use of a tripod to prevent camera shake. The cameraman also carries a silent camera (commonly an Arriflex), partly as a reserve but also for what are known as 'library' shots, meaning pictures of a street where a murder took place or a stately home that is to be auctioned. The cameraman may well go alone to take these shots. But increasingly cameramen employ a sound-on-film camera even for silent shots, because it will record the natural sound of street traffic or chirping birds and, though sound may not be needed at the time the film is shot, there may be a call for it later. Most frequently the camera is used on the shoulder, but the cameraman always has a tripod in the car, because if he has to have a camera on a cabinet minister in a conference-room for ten minutes it is simpler for him to put it on the tripod to ensure steady pictures, enabling him to sit down behind it in comfort. Nevertheless, if the cameraman has a steady hand, viewers cannot easily detect the difference between hand-held and tripod shots.

Black-and-white film has become outmoded and colour reversal film stock is now standard, the normal loading having a daylight speed of 80 ASA. The sound recordist's equipment, carried in the same car, includes, apart from the amplifier, a variety of stick, neck and throat microphones, plus headphones and a cassette recorder for use where additional sound is required.

For travelling abroad on an assignment the equipment used to be put into metal cases for safety, but nowadays fibre cases are used to save weight – and reduce excess baggage charges. Even so, the total weight taken by a two-man crew going abroad is around 160 kilos, which is the equivalent of two $12\frac{1}{2}$ stone men in weight, so it is like taking along two unconscious extra passengers. Crews used to split the load into ten to fourteen cases for easier handling, but this made it too easy for thieves to lift. Today they pack it into two or three cases, making it difficult for an airport sneak-thief to run off with one.

On arrival at an hotel much of the gear can be stored, and then drawn on as required. Even so, the crew is dependent on transport. Their first act on arrival is to try to hire a self-drive car, for drivers are not always keen to share the life of a television newsman. 'In Pakistan we had to go to war in a taxi every morning,' says a veteran ITN cameraman, Cyril Page, 'and the moment the taxi driver heard shooting ten miles away he would not go any further, so we had to take the gear off and start humping.'

Cameras are maintained to the highest possible standard in television maintenance departments, for it can be tricky when something goes wrong, particularly if it happens abroad. In Cyprus in 1974 ITN had a camera become non-operational because a driving band was affected by the heat. It took two days to get another camera out, because there were no direct flights operating to Cyprus, and it had to

Cyril Page with a modern Auricon film camera

be flown to Tel Aviv and onwards by charter aircraft.

Cyril Page recalls:

'In Biafra, where we all nearly got written off, we travelled about 200 miles in a Land-Rover through the bush where there was no road at all, and when I got the camera off to start work one of the transistors inside had broken and that camera was no use at all, so I had to shoot everything on a silent camera. We could not drive all the way back to Lagos to ask them to fix the camera, or pick up a telephone and ask someone to send another, so the only thing to do was to find another cameraman from someone like CBS which was not in direct opposition to us and ask to borrow his camera when he was not using it. This can be done in places like that. In the field it has been known that a guy says, "Well, I've got an extra 100 feet of film here that I shot but don't need – would you like it?" There is an awful lot of co-operation in the field between the old hands, despite the competition.'

Good and bad jobs

Yet the pace grows ever more killing. The old BBC newsreels were leisurely. Cyril Page remembers:

'We used to go away a lot, for a week or a fortnight and find stories. One would go to, say, Exeter to do a job at a toy manufacturer's and they would say, "Stay there and look around", and you would spend another couple of days there and come back with a package of four or five stories.'

Jobs like that are few and far between today. Page says:

'One of the nicest jobs I ever had was when I flew to Miami to meet John Fairfax when he rowed the Atlantic. That was more like a holiday than working. We used to like doing the old *Roving Reports* which were rather like travelogues. They got us away for a week and we would go somewhere and find a story and they were very popular.'

Today cameramen have to rush to get film on satellites. Despite the quality of the transmission considering the circumstances, cameramen are not keen on satellited material and prefer not to accept any head-office judgement on their films until the originals can be viewed in London. Unlike a current affairs team which normally includes a director, the cameraman of the two-man news crew is his own direc-tor. He decides the shots, where to zoom (pull in or out of close-up) or to pan (move the camera laterally). The reporter may decide the shape of the story, but it is the cameraman who creates the visual content. A reporter will say, 'I'm going to interview that person and where do you want me?' And the cameraman will say, 'I'd like you over there so I can get the background of that chimney.' Alternatively, a reporter may say, 'Can you get that picture in the background because I would like to turn round and refer to it.' The cameraman will provide the shot.

An umbrella protects the camera; the operator gets wet

Of course, film inserts in news programmes are short. It has to be a good interview to run more than two and a half minutes. It may be only a minute. There are occasions when film will run eight or nine minutes, but these are rare. In current affairs programmes the times are much longer. The worst job, by general consensus, is 'doorstepping' in Downing Street. Cameramen appealed to Edward Heath when he was premier for a room at No. 10 where they could wait, as is done at the White House where a bell rings when the President is emerging. In London cameramen may stand for five or six hours, perhaps in pouring rain, to get a shot lasting a few seconds of the Prime Minister or a visitor getting into a car. An alternative suggestion the newsmen put forward was to have a live television camera mounted on the nearby Colonial Office and lights fixed on the walls. This would cut out the need for cameramen milling about and attracting crowds of passers-by. But nothing has been done.

The longest-running story, on which more film has been expended than anything else, is Ulster. Crews have been going there in rotation for years now. It is not a popular job. Cameramen prefer what one called 'real wars' to Northern Ireland because, as he said, 'in a real war you know who your enemies are, and where they are'. But the main reason for their dislike of Ulster is not the danger but the boredom, the waiting in an hotel, unable to leave in case news arrives of an incident. Cyril Page buys Airfix kits and makes model aircraft to

Outside No. 10 – the Prime Minister speaks to the microphones

while away the time waiting for the next bomb blast, gun battle or murder.

One development in photography, brought about by television coverage in Belfast, where powerful lights could provoke violence, has been the use of an image intensifier, a device about two feet long attached to the camera in place of the normal lens, which enables it virtually to see in the dark. To be exact, a man invisible to the naked eye at eighty yards becomes so clear that the cameraman can count the buttons on his coat. This does not, of course, outmode the use of a lighting engineer, also known as an electrician or 'spark', on more conventional assignments. The cameraman decides whether he is likely to need the services of an electrician. This is not always easy to decide for, while a statesman may readily agree to be filmed in his garden or the street, a suspected criminal may agree to be photographed only on condition that he is shown in silhouette indoors. The lighting engineers of ITN travel in Ford Escorts carrying lamp-heads, battery packs and a battery charger, several stands and quartz lamps of from 250 to 800 watts, plus leads and accessories.

Lighting is one area in which the normally competitive BBC and ITN co-operate. If both arrive to film an interview, the one that arrives and sets up first will often leave the lighting until the opposition has also finished, both to avoid unnecessary work and to avoid losing the subject's goodwill by setting up twice. It should be noted in passing that, while most of the original television news cameramen came from the cinema newsreels (which closed down gradually as television gained in popularity), new routes are being established: from film editor to cameraman, electrician to sound recordist, and sound recordist to cameraman.

Chapter 7

Processing the news

There are three news programmes from ITN every weekday, but the major one and the longest one, on which most energy and resources are expended, is *News at Ten*. The producer of that programme arrives at the office at 10 am and works until 11 pm, though actually the day will have begun for him at the 'look-ahead' conference the previous afternoon. Immediately after the editor's 10.30 am conference the producer, who is also known, equally aptly, as the output editor, holds a conference with his own immediate team. They are a copy taster, who makes a first evaluation of agency tape messages, a chief sub-editor responsible for the bulletin's words and the timing of those words, and a chief sub (film) who monitors the film material. The producer depends upon these men because he cannot afford to stay in one place during the day. He has to be at his desk to read major stories as they arrive and to liaise with the chief sub about what is being written in the office, and he also has to spend some time in the cutting-rooms viewing the first rushes of film stories. If he loses touch with any aspect of the news processing operation the bulletin is liable to get out of shape.

At his morning meeting the producer devises a running order for the night's programme as though he were bringing it out at lunch-time. He knows that the running order will change as new stories break and promising stories collapse, but he must start establishing a format. It is a general rule that the most important story will be the lead or opener, whether or not it is exciting or visual. Television news has often led on subjects like inflation which do not lend themselves to dramatic film and will be boring to a large part of the audience, but the producer will choose the lead on merit. It would be simple to follow with the other stories in descending order of importance, but that would be liable to result in dull, non-illustrated stories followed by a second half of lighter-weight stories. Since the producer is building a show designed to entertain as well as inform, he works to create peaks and troughs as much as the writer of a drama or comedy script. The show should rise and fall like a human voice. Up at the opening, down, then up again at the close of the first half. Up at the opening of the second half, down, and up again at the end. These, of course, are just the main high and low spots. In practical terms it means that, after deciding the lead, he needs to place a strong story to kick off the second half of the programme. Then he will slot stories at the end of the first half and the end of the programme, though ITN normally attempts to close on a light note as an antidote to so much of the gloomy news that will have preceded it. Into this framework the producer slots other stories, some leading naturally from one to another. For example, two political stories may be linked together, but mindful of pace, he will intersperse some 'quickies' between them like gear-changes in a car.

There are several ways in which news can be presented on television: by cameras, live as it happens in the street or in the studio; in recorded pictures, on film or videotape; in words, by a newscaster or reporter addressing the viewers; or by stills, maps and graphics. The ideal is in pictures. But however the producer visualizes the show, he will have major tasks of selection and compression. Although *News at Ten* is nominally a half-hour programme, there are only $26\frac{1}{2}$ minutes left when the commercials at beginning, middle and end have been discounted. Deducting time for the opening titles and headlines and signing off at the end, the producer has no more than twenty-five minutes to work with and into that time it will be hard to cram eighteen or even seventeen minutes of visual material, for he must allow for leads in and out of the film material. So if he wants to devote perhaps six minutes to a scoop, some lesser stories must be pruned or discarded ruthlessly.

The producer goes to lunch at about 1.30 pm after watching *First Report* in case there is an interview that he feels will still have value for *News at Ten*, or he can spot a story suggesting a more detailed follow-up. Back at his desk at 2.30 or 3 pm he begins to get what David Phillips calls the plus and minus signs. The minus signs are items which are not standing up to their early promise or which look unlikely to arrive. The plus signs are the extra, unexpected stories that are coming in or expected stories that promise to be more exciting than had been anticipated.

Film and graphics

By this time film packages are arriving in the office. From airports and trysts with cameramen, motorcycle despatch riders deliver the cans of film to the processing laboratories. There films are hardened and developed for the first time to produce negatives which are washed and put into a second developing bath to produce a colour positive or print. They are washed again, bleached and fixed, the colours are stabilized and the prints are dried. The total time taken is normally less than forty minutes. The processing laboratories have a staff of about ten and are in operation from 9 am to 3 am next day, and even the gap in the early hours is sometimes filled with overtime work. Every day they handle around 12,000 feet of film.

From the laboratories the films move on to the film editors who will

A film editor at work

cut a film to manageable and coherent shape in fifteen to twenty minutes. Even when 1,000 feet of film arrive at 9 pm they will be processed and edited into a three- or four-minute package for *News at Ten* the same night and, to outsiders at least, the film is as well edited as if it had been in the office all day.

Scriptwriters for *News at Ten* report for work at about 2.30 pm, are briefed by the chief sub (film) and begin tailoring words to films and seeking out library film clips, still pictures and graphics where necessary to illustrate a story. Stock film and videotape are stored in the basement of ITN House. Every morning all the film and videotape of the previous day is sent to the library – the transmitted material and the cuts, and material that has not been touched. Transmitted film and tape are kept in their entirety. Other material to be retained is selected. The library also houses historic newsreel film acquired over the years from many sources and dating back long before the start of ITN.

The first purpose of the library is to service ITN and the UPITN agency, but it also provides material for the current affairs programmes of the ITV companies and television stations abroad. The original film or tape never leaves the library; a copy is always made, even when it is for use by ITN itself. A scriptwriter's requisition for stock film will normally be met within thirty minutes, says librarian David Warner. Complicated requests take longer, but film biographies of prominent people are held ready for use like the obituaries in a newspaper office. However, since they may be wanted on occasions other than the death of the subject, they are supposed to be referred to as 'profiles' rather than 'obits'. Every piece of film or tape is filed by date and the date is used as an index number; every shot is cross-indexed so that a meeting at Balmoral between the Queen and Harold Wilson is indexed under *Balmoral*, *Queen* and *Wilson H.*

More videotape than film is used in news bulletins today, though a lot of the tape started life as film. What has happened is that the film has been fed down the line from Scotland or Cyprus, or wherever it originated, and recorded in London. In the interests of quality the library always tries to get back the original film, after which the tape will be wiped for reuse.

In the graphics department the commonest request is for name captions to identify for viewers people appearing on screen during a programme. They are most often superimposed on the lower third of the screen and are then referred to as lower-frame supers. (When the wording fills the screen they are called full-frame supers.) To produce these captions for routine programmes a hot-press machine is used. A card 12 by 9 inches is put face upwards on a movable metal bed, and a thin sheet of plastic foil is placed over it. On this is placed metal type, face downwards. The bed is then moved under a hot plate and pressure is applied so that the heated type melts the foil and leaves a permanent impression. It takes only about three minutes to produce a simple caption and the graphics department at ITN, headed by Malcolm Beatson, produces about twenty-five a day, even though regularly recurring captions such as 'Peter Sissons, Industrial Editor' are kept on file.

On major programmes such as general election and budget days an electronic keyboard machine is used. On this, captions and messages can be punched out as easily as on a typewriter. They can be positioned in any part of the screen, rolled up it at variable speeds and moved from side to side. More importantly, the machine will also store captions. During the Apollo 11 moon landing a machine was programmed with nearly a thousand captions giving information identifying speakers and announcing what was happening. These captions were stored in the machine's memory bank. On the night, Frank Miles, who had studied the astronauts' voices as well as the operation itself, had only to give the operator a number and an appropriate caption was flashed on screen and this was done every fifteen seconds during the eleven-minute descent to the moon. Similarly, for budget programmes, the machine is fed with captions covering almost every possible tax variation.

Maps are also demanded for news programmes. The graphics

department has divided the world into sixty sections and keeps a stock of general-purpose maps of each of them, prepared on different scales. Paint, paper and dry transfer lettering can be added to the basic maps as required for special purposes. They are 20 by 25 inches in size, which is big enough to work on easily and also allows the director to pan a camera across the whole map and to zoom in as necessary on a particular area.

For showing weather forecasts and financial information and for some election results, magnetic units are commonly used. These graphics and diagrams and tables that may be devised to illustrate, say, rising prices or world shortages, may be either transmitted full screen or inlaid electronically into the blue Chromakey screen behind the newscaster in the studio.

The biggest demand for graphics comes at election times and during space missions. For elections the department creates a large studio scoreboard to show gains and losses, percentage swings and computer predictions. Sometimes the units are changed manually, but ITN has also used electromagnetic Solari equipment similar to that which changes the information on departure boards at large railway stations. For space missions they created 3D lunar dioramas upon which were placed models of the lunar module, the astronauts and their equipment.

The BBC's Sue Lawley with a 'swingometer' during the 1974 autumn election

Running order and script

At 4.30 pm the producer breaks off from the preparations for that day
to attend the look-ahead meeting to consider prospects for the following day. After that the pace begins to increase as he prepares for the
5.30 meeting, at which he must present his firm plans for the evening
show. By this time the early evening bulletin is in rehearsal in the
studio. The producer watches it before taking an early supper-break.
At 7 pm he is back, reminding the scriptwriters what he is expecting
from them and warning them of any problems such as legal traps. He
briefs the engineering and technical staff at the same time.

A final running order is produced – final except that it may be
scrapped if late news breaks. Production assistants and secretaries are
typing the script on carbonized paper. There are eight copies – the top
white one for the director and grey ones for the newscasters, because
television cameras do not like white. The running order, spaced
loosely over two pages, starts with the words, 'Titles/Bongs' (the
'bongs' being ITN shorthand for the headlines – from the sounds of
Big Ben, between which they are inserted). The items that follow are
numbered – from 1 to 22 in a typical day's running order. No. 1 is the
lead story and reads, let us say 'AG/ENERGY CUTS/CAPS/VARLEY FILM'.
This indicates it is to be introduced by Andrew Gardner, is about
energy cuts, and that there are captions to be superimposed followed
by a film interview with the Energy Secretary. No. 9 says 'AG/PRECOM'
and shows that Andrew Gardner will deliver the pre-commercial, the
teaser designed to persuade viewers to remain for the second half of
the programme after the commercial break, which lasts 2.05 minutes.
The final item, No. 22, which reads 'AG/TAILPIECE', is a twenty-second
humorous signing-off story, again from Gardner.

Production assistants annotate the timing of each item down the
right-hand side of the pages, together with the running total of time
elapsed at each story, plus, in the reverse order, the time remaining
after each story. The total may come out at twenty-eight minutes
thirty-five seconds, which is overlong and will have to be cut during
the rehearsal or actual performance.

The script follows. It is twenty-two pages long but the copy is well
spaced. First come the headlines – five items, the longest twelve words
and the shortest nine: 'The energy crisis – Mr Varley says slow down
and switch off. . . . At the Paris summit – an atmosphere of goodwill
towards Britain. . . . The HS 146 Airbus is to stay in cold storage . . .'
and so on. Alongside each headline is typed the method of illustration
– slides, still and film respectively in this case.

The next page begins: 'Good evening. The government have announced their plans to cut our fuel bill by £700 millions a year. . . .' It
is followed by captions that set out the main points of the government

plan. Then Eric Varley's words are set out as he has spoken them to the sound-on-film camera. It makes it easier for all concerned to follow the progress of the programme and to see where cuts can be made during the actual transmission if necessary, and it makes it possible for a newscaster to explain what should have been heard if the sound on the film fails.

Armed with running order and script, at 9.30 in theory but probably 9.40 in practice, *News at Ten* moves into the studio, and at this point the producer literally takes a back seat, behind the director of the programme. Only one person can drive a car and only one can drive a programme: the driving is the director's job, though the producer may have to take policy decisions and pass them on during the programme if a big story breaks.

Chapter 8
Presenting the news

The director links the journalistic and engineering staffs. His job is to bring together into a smooth-running show all the separate elements of the output, the newscasters and reporters in the studio, the lengths of film and videotape, the still pictures and graphics, and the live inserts from outside broadcast units, regional companies and satellite points.

There are four directors on duty at ITN every weekday, one allocated to each of the three programmes and the fourth to the outside broadcast unit. The *News at Ten* director arrives shortly before midday and begins by talking to the producer about the prospects for the show. In the hours that follow he liaises with the scriptwriters about the use of stills, graphics and stock film, his special concern being the visual aspect of the programme. He may direct the pre-recording in the studio of an insert for the programme, such as a report by the science correspondent involving the use of models, which it is deemed safer to have on videotape rather than showing live. He may carry out other chores, too, such as making a promotional trailer or directing the recording of an interview with a Member of Parliament requested by a regional company.

Eventually the director and his production assistant mark their scripts with the shots and the cameras to be used for each. There are normally four cameras in the studio (though eight will be used on election nights). Cameras one and two are used to screen the newscasters and any reporters appearing on the programme in the studio; cameras three and four show slides and graphics. Cameras one and two are special cameras for use with Chromakey, a system which enables films, tape, stills and slides to be shown as backgrounds behind the newscasters. It replaced Eidophor, which projected material on to a screen behind them. In the Chromakey system there is a blue rectangle behind them and films and slides are inlaid into the space electronically without actually appearing on the studio wall. The camera frames the newscaster and the blue patch while in the control room the vision mixer cuts in, say, a slide on camera three. Basically Chromakey operates by taking out the colour blue in the studio, which means that the newscaster cannot wear a blue tie or he would appear to have a slot between neck and navel. So newscasters never wear blue, though a reporter sometimes arrives in the studio in a blue suit, protesting that he was not expecting to have to go before the Chromakey camera. He then has to take off his jacket and borrow one of another colour. It is standard ITN policy to inlay a Chromakey background behind a reporter in the studio to give visual life to his report. At the BBC the system – known there as CSO (colour separation overlay) – was used until a change of presentation was introduced in 1975, to show a newsroom scene behind the newsreaders, who were in fact in a quite separate studio.

Black-and-white still pictures are mounted on card for showing by a camera, while any picture in colour is made into a slide. There are slide projectors on all the telecine machines and small ones in the studios, but anything that is to go on Chromakey behind the newscasters is put before a camera because it has to be framed accurately.

So, in allocating his cameras on the script, the director has to bear in mind that if he wants to use Chromakey to show Andrew Gardner live with a slide of Harold Wilson, and Reginald Bosanquet live with a slide of Edward Heath, he will need his four cameras.

Rehearsal

The director's main work starts with the rehearsal. There are two studios at ITN, but Studio Two is small and programmes normally originate from Studio One. However, on big occasions such as elections, both studios are used: Studio One becomes the election studio

In the News at Ten *studio – four cameras, two newcasters and teleprompter operator*

and Studio Two the general news studio. The director works on Studio Two and treats Studio One like an outside broadcast.

Normally there will be four cameramen in the studio (though the BBC operates its cameras by remote control). There will be two news-casters facing monitor screens recessed into their desks, surrounded by microphones, telephones and scripts, and with hairbrushes, tissues and lime-juice near to hand. There will be a floor manager, a caption changer, a slide projectionist and a PA to work the teleprompt mach-ine. The director takes his seat in a control-room above, facing a battery of monitor screens showing what is going out to the viewers, the shots available from cameras in the studio and shots available from cameras in other centres. On his right sits his production assis-tant; on his left, before a 3-foot wide bank of panel buttons, sits the vision mixer. The chief sub-editor sits next to the PA so that she can tell him how the timing is going, and the producer sits behind. There is a 'traction driver' who rolls film on the telecine machines by remote control, the technical supervisor of the day, the lighting, camera control and sound engineers, and behind them the script-writers.

Rehearsals are always rushed and frequently as much as half the programme cannot be rehearsed because it is not ready. A scriptwriter may still be working on one story. There may be a 'voice report' to come from a correspondent abroad, who has not had time to get to a television studio but can telephone from his home or hotel. The call may be booked for 9.50 pm, these telephoned reports being made on special lines called 'music lines' which provide superior quality with-out 'pips' or other interference – in theory at any rate. (If the sound quality is too bad to broadcast a writer has to produce a story saying 'Our correspondent tells us that . . .') Booking the call too early may mean that the reporter's information will be out of date by the time it is broadcast, so the calls are generally recorded a few minutes in advance of the programme. But sometimes they are made live, and when this happens the newscaster will often be seen talking to the reporter via a telephone on his desk, which makes more visual impact than if he were merely to listen to the reporter's voice while the screen showed a still picture of him or of some local landmark.

A satellite report may be booked for even later – perhaps ten min-utes into the programme. This applies particularly with correspon-dents in America, because at 10 pm in Britain it is only tea-time in the United States and the news is flowing. During the Watergate in-vestigation ITN took regular live transmissions from Washington and the satellite line was often available only at 10.10 pm and then for only a limited time because other organizations would be queueing up for it. This meant that the previous story in the news had to be timed to finish by 10.10, so that the newscaster could say 'And now, over to Washington' and avoid wasting any time.

If he has had time the reporter will have sent a Telex earlier in the day suggesting illustrations that may be relevant, so that they can be prepared in advance. However, the most the director can do is to rehearse as much of the newscasters' material and as many pieces of film as possible, though, because of the pressure of time, the director will sometimes run only the first few words and then say, 'Right, that's enough. On to the next story.' The director will, however, try to rehearse anything complicated like the animation of a model or a reporter's use of a light pen. The chief thing he gets out of the rehearsal is a check on timing and camera shots and the use of Chromakey.

Diana Edwards-Jones, once a stage manager in the theatre, later a studio floor manager at ITN and now one of the country's most experienced news directors, says:

'Sometimes you have to stop when you have only got to story fifteen and there are five more stories to come, because sometimes you don't even get the script until the titles are going on. One never goes down with a complete script, because the writers are up against it and they are waiting for film to be out of the labs and edited.

'I have actually done *News at Ten* without a rehearsal at all, other than just going through the camera shots without the newscasters reading anything. That usually happens when there is a major change because something happens at 9.30 pm. Actually, it is much easier if big news comes at a minute to transmission, because you have no time then to alter anything before the start. You do the headlines as they were written and then the newscaster says, "Good evening. We have just had news that ... and we'll be bringing you a report on that later", and then you carry on with what you have got and rejig the programme while on the air.'

Directing the programme

As 10 pm approaches the rehearsal must end. The clock-watching PA announces how many minutes or seconds the show is over or under time, the producer decides on the cuts or additions, and the chief sub makes the adjustments. The director and his assistants are watching the monitor screens. Film and tape are on the telecine and videotape machines ready to roll. There are four VTR machines normally and four telecine machines, one for slides and three for film. The director's PA goes into her countdown, 'Five ... four ... three ...', Big Ben starts to boom and the newscaster begins the headlines.

The brief illustrations to each of the headlines bring an immediate test of the directorial team's skill, because both VTR and telecine machines need time to run up to their correct playback speeds and

Award-winning news director Diana Edwards-Jones

they have to be started several seconds before the newscaster reaches the appropriate point if the director is to be able to cut smoothly to the right picture. From then on the director is working flat out calling the shots to the vision mixer. If all goes well the programme cuts smoothly from newscaster to tape, film, captions and maps, to a live report from a provincial city, to more film and back to the newscaster. The worst sin in the director's book is having a blank screen for a moment – 'going to black' as it is called in the profession. Fortunately it happens rarely.

The director has a talk-back system, heard through headphones or earpieces by key people like newscasters, cameramen and floor manager, videotape operators and master control, which sends the programme on its way to the transmitter. To pass on a quick message, anyone in the control-room can speak over the director's shoulder into the microphone. For instance, the PA can warn, 'You've one minute to go' towards the end of a studio interview. And in the control room the staff live by the clock. The PA uses a stop-watch and there is also a back-timing clock showing time remaining, as opposed to time elapsed. Yet there is little drama. When a piece of film is running, although it has to be watched in case of a break, the team take the opportunity to make any cuts necessary. If the PA says the programme is going to overrun by a few minutes, the producer will make a snap decision on what to cut, the chief sub will amend the script and the newscasters will be told. The producer has a direct telephone to the newscasters for use in real emergencies.

When a big story breaks, the producer may seek permission to extend the news. This is not asked lightly, because it causes complications in ITV's federal structure of fourteen regions, and these will not necessarily be showing the same programme or even programmes of the same length after the news. There are also advertisements booked to appear at a fixed time. To extend the programme ITN appeals to ITV's master control which, during the week, is situated at Thames Television, the London weekday programme company, and at weekends at London Weekend Television.

Overruns must be of either two or six minutes' duration. The news cannot be extended for three or five minutes. So the producer asks for either two minutes, which will be simply added to the programme, or six minutes, in which case another commercial break will be included. If master control thinks that ITN has a good case he will pick up a red telephone and warn the network of the change in timing. In practice, since ITN is highly regarded and never seeks extra time without good reason, permission is never refused, though for convenience a regional company may decide to tape the overrun and transmit it later.

Eventually, when the programme comes to an end, the team relax, drained. Diana Edwards-Jones says:

'There is more pressure on a news director than on any other television director. The news is live for a start, whereas most programmes are taped, and there is so much happening. Most places have only about six monitors, but this place is like Cape Canaveral – on an election programme there are thirty-six monitors. Sometimes at the end of a show you think, that went all right, and you are shattered because technically it was very hairy. But to be quite honest, half the time I don't know what it was like because one has been concentrating so hard on getting everything in and out at the right places.

'We extended quite a lot over President Nixon's departure. I think when I worked it out I had done the equivalent of twelve *News at Ten*s in three days. Sometimes I'm so shattered by the end of the show that I can't stand up. Sometimes I have been physically sick. Sometimes we just sit there and ask, "Why do we do it?" That is why we have the shift system – three days on, then a week-end off, then another three days and eventually six days off.'

After the programme the team remains on standby until about 11 pm in case of any repercussions or a news-flash. A late sub-editor will stay at his desk to watch for a major story breaking, because ITN never closes. However, if anything breaks after 11 pm he will ring the transmission controllers of the programme companies and it is left to them to put out a flash. At the BBC a duty newsreader will announce it from a desk in the newsroom.

Chapter 9
The front men

Newscasters and newsreaders are personable men, but few could be said to have the clean-cut handsomeness of male models. Most are middle aged. Yet to the general public they are as much show-business stars as are actors and singers. They feature in the gossip columns. They are regularly invited to open charity fêtes and business conferences and to appear in panel games (which some of them do). They are pressed to endorse products in advertising campaigns, which they do not do, for they have to be above suspicion of being susceptible to any outside interests. They also receive fan mail. One woman wrote to Gordon Honeycombe as follows: 'I kneel down when you are reading the news and passionately kiss the screen.' And in a letter to Richard Whitmore a schoolgirl declared: 'I think you are so gorgeous, I really love you. I cry myself to sleep on the nights when you do not read the news.' They would not be human if they were not flattered by the letters but, working in a world of journalists rather than entertainers, they are also embarrassed and wary of answering letters seeking advice on business or social problems. It is not easy to compose replies to inadequate and lonely people that are neither so cool as to hurt nor so kind as to encourage fantasies. They also have to be on their guard when appearing on screen because, as Andrew Gardner says, women write suggesting a newscaster scratches his nose or ear as a signal that he has received a letter and reciprocates the sentiments in it.

Not all the letters are from admirers. Some are remarkably offensive – about their diction, for example: 'Dear Whitmore, would you kindly have the courtesy not to emphasize pronouns.' Or their personal appearance: 'Cut your hair and try to look less like a woman.' Or even about the news they introduce: 'When you are on, it is nothing but strikes, riots and disasters. Can't you find some cheerful news for a change?' What worries the newsmen more is when they are accused of having displayed political or moral bias by an alleged vocal inflection or facial expression. In some ways they correspond to newspaper columnists in that they are the well-paid and publicized personalities who give the programme some of its character. But newspaper columnists are generally paid to parade their personal opinions and prejudices as forcefully as possible, while television newsmen are required to keep their own views to themselves. Normally it is only while interviewing in the course of a programme that they question statements or views, and then it is to play the devil's advocate in the pursuit of objectivity or balance by reminding the public that there may be another point of view or interpretation.

Yet their personalities register, probably because the first requirement of a newscaster, it is generally agreed, is authority. This authority comes from confidence, which in turn comes from experience in dealing with the crises that occur in the studio and also from a wide knowledge of current affairs in general and a thorough knowledge of the specific stories to be related. Reginald Bosanquet claims that two other qualities required are relaxation ('because you are in the viewer's drawing-room') and humour ('because most of the news is so depressing that you need some light relief').

Personality was avoided in British television journalism before the arrival of ITN in 1955, because the BBC feared that a human touch might lead to the objectivity of its bulletins being questioned. The qualities ITN sought from its first newscasters were set out when the posts were advertised in June 1955. The advertisement read: 'The job would involve helping to prepare, and appearing on screen to deliver, the daily news bulletins for the new Independent Television service. No previous broadcasting experience necessary. Requirements: sound knowledge of current affairs, ability to think on feet, good presence. The work might appeal to a barrister thinking of giving up practice. The post would carry a good salary.'

Robin Day, one of the original newscasters, was, as already mentioned, a barrister, though he had practised for only a year. Christopher Chataway, the first newscaster to be seen on screen, was also the first to leave. He decided he did not want to continue with nightly television and, after six months, joined BBC's *Panorama* team, leaving eventually to become a Conservative MP. Robin Day, who left ITN six months before the general election of 1959, to stand, unsuccessfully, as a Liberal candidate, followed him to *Panorama*. Chataway was succeeded by Ludovic Kennedy, a writer and broadcaster probably best known then as the husband of Moira Shearer, the ballet dancer. He stayed two years before moving to *This Week*. Many newsmen have made the move from news to current affairs.

Today's newscasters and newsreaders come from a wide range of backgrounds. ITN's unflappable Andrew Gardner, 6 feet 5 inches tall, began in radio broadcasting in Africa in 1956 and was one of the first reporters in the Congo during the 1960 massacres. He returned to Britain and joined ITN in 1961 and says he is happy to be studio-based as long as he is involved in the preparation of the news he is to present. Reginald Bosanquet has known no other employer but ITN, becoming a newscaster in 1957, two years after joining the original backroom team from Oxford University. Between 1957 and 1967, however, he visited fifty-two countries reporting for ITN's news background programme *Roving Report* and news bulletins. Gordon

Andrew Gardner

Reginald Bosanquet

Honeycombe was an actor and now combines newscasting with a highly successful career as a novelist. Leonard Parkin had an orthodox newspaper background. He joined a weekly newspaper from school and went on to the *Yorkshire Evening News* in Leeds. Later he worked as a radio reporter, and in 1954 he became one of BBC Television's original reporters. He has seen most of the world's trouble spots. Robert Kee, a wartime bomber pilot who spent three years as a prisoner of war, has been in television journalism since 1958, working for *This Week* and his own series *Robert Kee Reports*. He joined ITN to introduce *First Report* when it began in 1972.

At the BBC, Peter Woods is a Fleet Street veteran. He jumped with the paratroops in the Suez landings for a newspaper story and has worked as a reporter for both ITN and the BBC. After wartime service as a naval officer, Richard Baker was briefly a teacher and an actor before becoming a radio announcer in 1950. Kenneth Kendall

Richard Baker

Peter Woods

Angela Rippon

was also formerly a teacher and a radio announcer.

Although both television news organizations employ women reporters, there have been few women newscasters. Barbara Mandell was an ITN newscaster in 1955 before ITV achieved national coverage, and in 1960 the BBC used Nan Winton to read the national news. Sir Geoffrey Cox expressed his willingness to consider a woman newscaster when he launched *News at Ten* but was unable to find one he regarded as suitable. It has been widely held that women do not have the authority to present news of major importance. A BBC audience research poll found that 41 per cent were against, which was the majority. The most interesting discovery made by the poll was that men were mostly in favour of a woman newsreader, and it was women who were generally opposed to one. However, in 1975 Angela Rippon became a regular newsreader after two years as a BBC Television News reporter and previous experience as a reporter for newspapers and Westward Television.

The newscaster's work

The public tend to think that newscasters work only thirty minutes a day. In fact, *News at Ten* newscasters arrive at Wells Street at about 4.30 pm, or earlier if they have correspondence to attend to or interviews to give. First, they brief themselves on what has been happening and the general prospects for the bulletin. At 5.30 pm they attend the editor's meeting at which the shape of the bulletin is decided. They watch the early evening news and take a break from 6 to 7 pm. Another meeting with the producer follows, at which writers are assigned to stories. From this point on the pace quickens. They may be asked to write stories or to prepare for a live interview during the bulletin. One job is to write the headlines – the 'bongs'. Another task is to write the pre-commercial, designed to encourage viewers to sit through the commercial break for the second half of the programme. A third task is to write the tailpiece, if there is to be one. The theory is that a humorous tailpiece should be in the teller's own words because, if he doesn't find it funny, he will never convince viewers that it is. Newscasters are selective about tailpieces because genuinely amusing ones are rare, but they would like one every night and they always look out for them.

Copy is flowing fast by this time and the newscasters read it carefully. At ITN they can change the wording where they think it necessary. Basically they examine it for two things. First, that it has been written for speaking rather than reading. A writer under pressure may incorporate inverted phrases from an agency message that read well enough in print but are unnatural in speech. Relative clauses are a particular bugbear with newscasters and they will generally remove them. Second, they check it for accuracy. Reginald Bosanquet says:

'I regard myself as entirely responsible for everything I say on the programme. If a fact is wrong I regard that as my responsibility. I get all the newspapers and I read current affairs books and watch current affairs programmes. If I want to alter something I can alter it, but the corollary of this is that I take responsibility for what I say and it's no use complaining "Somebody got that wrong".'

The newscasters also take the opportunity to ensure that they can pronounce all the proper names in the bulletin. The BBC has a special unit to advise on pronunciation, because the local style often differs from the generally accepted one. This did not, however, prevent one newsreader from pronouncing Tucson, Arizona, as it is spelt, nor another from pronouncing the second part of Sir Alec Douglas-Home's surname to rhyme with Rome. At ITN it is left to the newscasters to establish correct or acceptable pronunciation.

The time arrives when the newscasters move into the studio for rehearsals and the programme itself. They have copies of the script in front of them and the same script is also fed through a teleprompter and displayed on screens beneath the cameras. When the BBC began television news the reader had only a script. (Robert Dougall once dropped all the pages and began reading with only the first folio in front of him.) ITN had teleprompters from the start, but the first machines needed a special typewriter and special paper and it took time to make alterations. Modern machines use ordinary typewriters and narrow rolls of paper, and amendments can be made quickly with scissors and a glue pen. But if a newscaster follows a teleprompter slavishly, viewers will see his eyes flickering from left to right and he will be in difficulties if the prompter breaks down. So most newscasters use both prompter and script and switch their glance regularly from one to the other.

The final running order, they say at ITN, is firm – until it changes. It has been changed just before 10 o'clock while the programme is being counted down on to the air – and changed again during the course of the programme. For example, although the attempt to kidnap Princess Anne in the Mall in 1974 happened earlier in the evening, details were still flooding in, and witnesses were being brought into the studio for live interviews after the programme had started.

In the early days of newscasting the presenter relied for late information on messages slipped on to his desk. Later it became customary to communicate instructions by a telephone placed in front of him. A break in a piece of film or a suddenly blank screen would be followed by the sight of an agonized link-man and then the sound of the telephone, which the newscaster would snatch up in search of an explanation. Many viewers remember a bizarre incident when Michael Aspel was reading a BBC news bulletin. The telephone was heard to ring, and went on ringing, but he was unable to find it! A studio cleaner had tidied it away in a drawer of his desk.

But, since *News at Ten* started, newscasters have worn 'deaf-aids', hearing-pieces modelled to their own ears and, when worn in the ear away from the camera, virtually invisible. Through the deaf-aid the director gives news of changes and on-air cuts, such as telling the newscaster in the middle of a story to drop the third paragraph. It is also used for giving the newscaster the count-down into film or videotape inserts, earlier signalled by cue lights. Sound film runs for six seconds before it appears on screen; six seconds at three words per second means that the film has to start running eighteen words back into the story preceding it. The deaf-aids of both newscasters carry the same messages, so while Reginald Bosanquet is reading a story he may be hearing instructions being given to Andrew Gardner. To an outsider it is incomprehensible that anyone can read a major news story while a voice is speaking in his ear, but Bosanquet says, 'You get used to it. It is very good training for cocktail parties. I can carry on a conversation with one person at a party and be listening to another person some distance away. A newscaster is a classic example of a schizophrenic. What the deaf-aid is doing to my ear-drum is another matter. Andrew and I fear we will be stone deaf by the time we are fifty, but we reckon we'll be dead by then anyway.'

As to job satisfaction in newscasting, Reginald Bosanquet says:

'I'm one of those people who always enjoy being informed ahead of other people and I like the feeling that I'm capturing the public's attention. And then we are the only part of television that is live, virtually everything else is on tape. The best programmes are the ones where something actually happens while you are on the air. Not only does this make the adrenalin go round faster – this is what it's all about, this is what television is, and this is what you need to involve the viewer in, this feeling that anything could happen and might, and when it does you must try and communicate your sense of excitement.

'My ideal programme is one in which at one minute to ten we tear up the entire running order and go over to some fantastic event like the House of Commons on fire. When the Israelis were shot at the Olympic Games I came in about 4.45 pm and they said to me, "You're on the air – open-ended", and people were shoving at me bits of scripts written on the backs of envelopes and bits of videotape and bits of film. I think we stayed on the air until about a quarter past six and it was terrific. Television news is being present at the event.'

Great occasions

In current affairs series the trend has been away from permanent front

men to reporters introducing their own stories. Partly this is to stream-
line the programmes and give them more urgency; and partly it is
because the programmes, with exceptions like *Weekend World*, introduced by Peter Jay, have moved away from a magazine format to
covering a single issue in each edition, making a link-man unnecessary.

In the years when *Panorama* enjoyed its greatest prestige its resident
anchor-man was Richard Dimbleby, whose personal popularity added
greatly to its viewing figures. A distinguished radio correspondent
during the war, Dimbleby established himself on television in the post-
war years as the country's supreme commentator on national events.
He described for the nation the coronation ceremony in Westminster
Abbey in 1953, the first state opening of Parliament to be televised in
1956, and the funeral of Sir Winston Churchill in 1965. That was his
last great occasion; he was dying of cancer. Some came to mock him
for being sycophantic and reverential about royalty, but no one could
match him in his choice of words to describe the colour, pageantry
and ritual of a state occasion. And the mass of the public loved him.
One of the reasons the BBC invariably captured the largest audience
for these events was the magic of Dimbleby. Beside him, other commentators seemed like substitutes from the reserves. At a memorial
service for him in Westminster Abbey, the former Archbishop of

David Dimbleby

Canterbury, Lord Fisher, said: 'Richard Dimbleby established a new art and a new profession of communicating to the people by a commentary the outward form and the inward meaning of great occasions, both in Church and State.'

The name of Dimbleby has continued in current affairs pro-

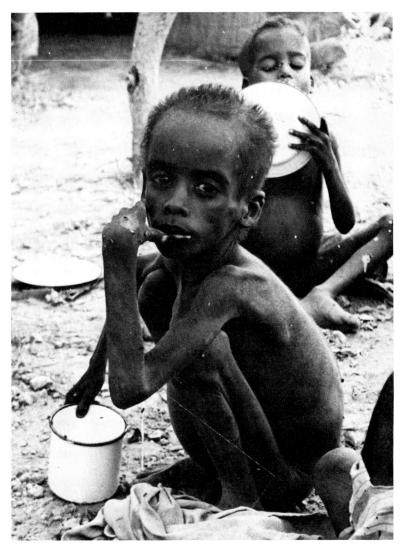

Starving child in the Ogaden desert region of Ethiopia

Jonathan Dimbleby (left) in Ethiopia

grammes. David Dimbleby, Richard's elder son, took his father's old chair in the *Panorama* studio in 1966 to introduce a special edition on cancer, and in 1974, on *Panorama*'s twenty-first birthday, he succeeded to his father's old job as resident link-man on the programme. By this time he had established his own reputation in programmes like *The Dimbleby Talk-in*. He had also done some commentaries; but his coverage of a visit by President Nixon to Britain in 1969 caused a row. The storm was over allegedly cynical remarks he made about 'the road show' and 'expensively hired press secretaries whose job is to disguise the truth'. Dimbleby declined to apologize but the BBC did, in a public announcement saying it greatly regretted 'remarks which were unfortunately inappropriate'. And Dimbleby ceased to do commentaries, declaring that if he did them in the way of his father, he sounded as though he was parodying him.

Meanwhile his brother Jonathan had made his name on Thames Television's *This Week*. In 1973 he won an award named after his father for the year's most important personal contribution to factual television, a programme on famine in Ethiopia which led to more than £1½ million being raised in Britain towards its relief.

Alastair Burnet

ITV eventually found a man for the big occasions in Alastair Burnet. He did not commentate on royal activities but fronted the network's coverage of general elections, budgets and space missions formidably, as a result of which ITV began to split the viewing figures on these occasions more equally with the BBC. Formerly a leader writer on the *Glasgow Herald*, Burnet was ITN's political editor from 1963 to 1965, when he became Editor of *The Economist*, but he continued as the spearhead of ITN's coverage of major national and international news. His great strength was his ability to ad-lib with authority in unscripted programmes. On general election nights he scorned the use of notes, which he said took too long to use, relying on his knowledge and memory. With the Apollo shots he played the man in the street, seeking information from the experts. In 1970 he was due to front the budget coverage when the Apollo 13 mission ran into trouble and he found himself fronting a combined budget and Apollo programme. Consequently he presented a programme which went on until 4 am, bringing the latest news of the spacemen and answering telephoned queries from viewers, and he stayed before the cameras until the 'burn' that brought the astronauts around the back of the moon and out of immediate danger. By then he had worked fifteen hours non-stop, only four hours less than during the 1969 moon-landing programme when the studio temperature reached the nineties.

When the BBC won Burnet away from ITN in 1972 it was a blow to ITV. In 1974 he became Editor of the *Daily Express* and announced his retirement from regular television work. But in 1976 he returned to ITV.

Chapter 10

Current affairs

Alongside the growth of the news has come the development of current affairs programmes, providing greater depth in the reporting, clarifying and evaluating of issues of the day. They are the equivalent of the features pages in newspapers. A distinction should be made between current affairs programmes and documentaries. Any factual programme longer than a news item can be classed as a documentary, but documentaries need not be topical. They can deal, and have dealt, with such subjects as the breeding of shire horses and battles of World War II – though John Edwards, who is responsible for documentaries and current affairs at Thames Television, comments, 'I don't think I would OK any documentary programme that had no relevance to life today.' However, current affairs programmes *must* be concerned with the topical and immediate, with issues that directly affect or concern the public. That leaves plenty of scope, for the issue need not be important or serious. A *This Week* programme asked, 'How cruel are talent contests?' A *Talk-in* sought to establish whether Uri Geller's spoon-bending was caused by the use of mental powers or conjuring tricks. Both subjects were creating discussion in the homes of Britain at the time they were shown, but neither could have justified the time in a news bulletin.

Current affairs series

In the thirties the nearest thing to a current affairs series was *Picture Page*, a magazine devoted to cosy chats with celebrities from tennis champions to aviators. After the war came discussion programmes such as *In the News*, which had more edge, but current affairs programmes were generally still studio-based.

An American series led the way. It was *See It Now*, a weekly thirty minutes produced by Fred W. Friendly and anchored by Edward R. Murrow, who had won fame for his coverage of the London blitz for American radio. The first programme on a November Sunday in 1951 took viewers to Korea, but complemented the news in that, instead of depicting fighting, it showed men of the 19th Infantry's Fox Company eating, sleeping and waiting. Each man stepped before the cameras, identifying himself by name and home town.

A year later the BBC began a monthly series called *Special Enquiry*, presented by Robert Reid, the Features Editor of the *News Chronicle*. Its first report was on slum housing in Glasgow, and subsequent programmes tackled discrimination against coloured people, smoke pollu-

Panorama's *picture of spaghetti harvesting in Switzerland*

tion and food hygiene. The series used film crews and reporters. *Panorama*, the oldest of current affairs series still running, began a year later. But in 1953 it was a fortnightly general purpose magazine subtitled 'a reflection on the contemporary scene' and it evoked little enthusiasm until it introduced Malcolm Muggeridge as an interviewer of the famous. In 1955, as ITV began, it was relaunched as a weekly peak-time programme concentrating on events of international importance and Richard Dimbleby was brought in as link-man to lend it weight. It went on to achieve a prestige unequalled in British television. Cabinet ministers and MPs came to the *Panorama* studio when bidden. It established a classic current affairs format of a film report followed by a studio discussion and never shirked tackling dull subjects if they merited its attention – though the *Panorama* item best remembered by many viewers is still the 1957 April Fool's Day one in which Dimbleby introduced a spoof about spaghetti trees. Guided to success by Michael Peacock, later Editor of BBC Television News, it made the television reputations of many, including Woodrow Wyatt, Robert Kee, Francis Williams and James Mossman. With David Dimbleby, it still concerns itself with major topics at home and abroad.

ITV's answer to *Panorama* was *This Week*, founded in 1956 by Associated Rediffusion, then the London weekday programme com-

pany. It was, and is, only a thirty-minute programme, and in its deter-
mination not to bore viewers it presented originally a hectic half-hour,
packing in half a dozen topics ranging on one occasion from poly-
gamy to black magic. Brian Connell was its best-known anchor-man
until 1963, after which it was left to each reporter to introduce his own
story. Today, presented by Thames Television, it covers only one story
in each edition, largely because of the increased length of the news
bulletins. Yet it avoids categorization and will follow a programme on
the political situation in Greece with an inquiry into rape.

Granada's *World in Action* introduced a new style when it began in
1963 under Tim Hewat, a forceful Australian journalist. There was no
link-man and no reporter was seen; there were no studio discussions
and commentary was limited to a voice-over. The tone was aggressive,
the matter sensational and its specialities were profiles and exposés.
Hewat's first programme was on the atomic arms race and his tabloid
newspaper approach was seen immediately; he had actors playing
Kennedy and Khrushchev scowling at each other through a forest of
missiles. In recent times under different producers the format has
become more flexible – for example, there have been studio discussions – but it has remained sensational in its investigative journalism.
Typically, in 1974, it brought to Britain Ben Hunter who advertises
homeless children to prospective foster parents on American
television, put him to work with British children and asked, 'Would
this technique be acceptable here?'

The number of current affairs series has grown in the last decade,
but each has been designed for a particular niche. BBC1 established
Nationwide as an early evening programme on domestic affairs five
nights a week, introduced by Michael Barratt and Frank Bough and
linking London with 11 provincial news centres. *Tonight*, reintroduced
in 1975 as a late-night weeknight programme, succeeding *Midweek*
(which succeeded *Twenty-Four Hours*) has concerned itself with the
day's international and domestic events. *Talk-in*, on Friday evenings,
conducted in turn by Robin Day and David Dimbleby, has offered an
opportunity to question one or more guests each week. On BBC2 in
The Money Programme, Alan Watson and others have covered aspects
of finance from shop-floor to boardroom level, from charities to taxa-
tion, while in *Europa* Derek Hart has shown how events are seen by
other European television organizations. On ITV, *Weekend World*, a
news analysis programme chaired by Peter Jay, was introduced at
lunch-time on Sundays as a serious newspaper of the screen. The IBA
claimed: 'The difference between *Weekend World* and *News at Ten* is
roughly the difference between "What?" and "Why?"'. *News at Ten*
explains what has happened and when and where; *Weekend World*'s
task is to say why it happened and what may happen because of it and

Brian Widlake (second left) presenting The Money Programme

Peter Jay

Cliff Michelmore presenting Tonight *in 1957*

Alan Whicker interviewing a Brighton pier dweller for Tonight

where it all fits into the overall picture.'

Along the way there have been many programmes which are no longer seen. One of the most mourned was the BBC's original *Tonight* programme which began in 1957 when the so-called 'toddlers' truce' – a close-down between 6 and 7 pm so that mothers could get children to bed – was ended. Donald Baverstock, a Welsh ex-schoolteacher, was given forty minutes of this time five nights a week for the programme, which was linked by Cliff Michelmore. It squabbled with *Panorama* over cabinet ministers and *Monitor* over artists, but its main material consisted of stories from its roving reporters. Fyfe Robertson, Trevor Philpott and others came to it after the collapse of the magazine *Picture Post*, and Alan Whicker joined it from the Exchange Telegraph news agency. It had a light touch to fit the early evening time, relished the eccentric and bizarre and ended with a topical calypso.

Equally mourned – at least by the staff of ITN – were the current affairs programmes which they began in 1957. First came *Roving Report*, which varied in length from fifteen to thirty minutes, was sometimes a magazine and sometimes devoted to one story. It never had a regular link-man and was introduced by its own reporters. Typical was a visit which Tom St John Barry paid to Lapland to visit the Post Office at Kiruna where letters addressed to Santa Claus are received and answered. It led in 1964 to *ITN Reports*, a weekly thirty-minute programme which became in 1966 *Reporting '66*. ITN used the time to report news events more fully and vividly than it could do in its regular bulletins. Its reporters flew with American combat pilots in Vietnam, patrolled the Malacca Straits with the Royal Navy, crouched under a Chinese bombardment in Quemoy, climbed the Radfan mountains in Aden with commandos. But these and other ITN supplementary programmes died in 1967 when the company surrended them to achieve the extra time to start *News at Ten*.

The satire boom of the early sixties brought a new element into current affairs. It began in 1962 with *That Was the Week That Was*, part light entertainment, part current affairs, fathered by ex-*Tonight* men including Donald Baverstock and introduced by the hitherto unknown David Frost. It commented on news events late on Saturday nights with songs sung by Millicent Martin, sketches performed by Roy Kinnear and Eleanor Bron and cartoons by Timothy Birdsall. Nothing was apparently sacred to *TW3* and its successor, *Not So Much a Programme, More a Way of Life*; it swiped at politicians, parsons and businessmen alike, and it caused such waves of protest that at one time Sunday newspapers ran the number of complaints about the previous night's programme like the football league tables.

There have been, and are today, many other programmes concerning themselves with aspects of current affairs, though not necessarily transmitted in that category. Among them have been interview and chat-show programmes such as David Frost's interview with Cardinal Heenan about the Pope's encyclical on birth control, his investigation into the Ronan Point disaster and his inquiry into Rolf Hochhuth's anti-Churchill play *Soldiers*. More recently, in 1975, Frost reintroduced himself with a new chat-show entitled *We British*. Bernard Braden's *On the Braden Beat* mixed pioneering consumer protection advice with light entertainment. A books programme concerned with a book on an issue of the day, a motoring magazine discussing reasons for the rising price of petrol, a science programme about a new form of medical treatment, or a religious programme on gambling could often have been transmitted equally validly as current affairs.

One type of supplementary news programme that has decreased is the outside broadcast of ceremonies and displays. Once television covered events like the Lord Mayor's Show and the Chelsea Flower Show in London at length. To some extent the novelty value has gone, but there is another reason for the decline. Until 1972 hours of television were restricted by the government, but outside broadcasts

A controversial Frost interview – with Enoch Powell in 1969

(within certain limits) did not count against the permitted hours. Paradoxically, when television was freed from restrictions, outside broadcasts lost much of their appeal for the television organizations.

The current affairs team

A current affairs team in the field is usually considerably larger than the news team of reporter, cameraman and sound recordist. Apart from the reporter the current affairs team will normally have two cameramen (a senior and his assistant), two sound recordists, a director and his production assistant, plus a researcher and possibly a lighting electrician. It is not unknown to have a team of thirteen. News reporters accustomed to travelling light view these numbers with some disdain, but the current affairs team may be expected to produce a definitive report of thirty minutes or more compared with a two and a half minute story by the news team. The size of the unit is laid down in agreements with the film union, although in a war zone (and for this purpose Ulster is so classed) the current affairs programme is allowed to send a 'one and one' crew of cameraman and sound recordist like a news programme.

Because of the manpower and money committed when a current affairs team decides to make a programme, a researcher (usually a university graduate hoping to become a reporter or producer) is sent ahead to investigate the possibilities and to make arrangements, so that the unit can set off with a draft script and a filming schedule. When it arrives the researcher will set up new arrangements for the reporter and cameraman while the rest of the team are out filming. The researcher is a junior member of the team but has to take some unenviable decisions. He or she may be sent to Israel to see if a proposed story will stand up: if he reports 'It's on' he is committing the programme to an expenditure of perhaps £12,000. Current affairs programmes are not cheap. (Another union agreement stipulates first-class air travel on journeys of more than a thousand miles.) As one producer put it: 'If companies were run by people purely concerned with profits I don't think they would regard current affairs as a very good thing to invest in.'

This Week has a producer with a staff of four reporters, four film directors and crews, one studio director and five researchers, so it could field four separate teams, but it is seldom that there will be work on four stories at the same time because some programmes require long periods of research. For instance, a researcher may have to work on a project for as long as eight months. In some circumstances, however, virtually all may be on the road. To cover fighting in the Middle East *This Week* once sent three teams comprised of about thirteen people.

Normally, in any given week, one film is being made and another is being edited. The gestation period for a *This Week* film is about three weeks. A researcher may be sent to, say, Ethiopia for ten days. Then the team follows and films for ten days, and editing may take another ten days. But it is dangerous to have many ready-made programmes on the shelf because they can be outdated by events. *This Week* has, in fact, a fairly small staff and other current affairs programmes have different staffing techniques. *World in Action*, for example, uses reporters who also act as producers.

The current affairs reporter has more time to devote to a story than a news reporter, but the pressures are not necessarily lighter. The news reporter files a fresh story every day and, for better or worse, is finished with it; he does the best he can in the time available. Next day he may move on to something else. The current affairs reporter may have to stay with a story for three weeks, striving to clean it up completely and hoping that the time will be justified by the end result. He may see news reporters shipping their reports to an airport each day while he can only count the number of usable minutes achieved; he cannot call a halt until he has reached the end of his filming schedule. John Edwards, who has been a reporter for both news and current affairs programmes, claims that current affairs calls for a greater ability. He says:

'I think very few news reporters could sustain a half-hour programme as the current affairs reporter has to be able to do. And the current affairs programme, by virtue of the longer time available, should have better film, better edited, and provide a better assessment than a news operation. The worst sort of current affairs programme is just a long, boring version of the news.'

Chapter 11
In the regions

Apart from the national news and current affairs programmes, television also offers regionalized programmes, devoted to local news and to issues which would not normally interest the whole country. The chief time for these is 6 pm, after the early evening national news, but there are other slots around lunch-time and late at night. ITV has always featured regional programmes because it was planned from its start in 1955 as a federation of areas served by independent programme companies. Today, as noted earlier, there are fourteen regions, served by fifteen companies (London has two – Thames Television providing programmes from Monday morning until 7 pm on Friday, and London Weekend Television providing them from then until close-down on Sunday). The other regions in descending order of viewing population are: the Midlands (covered by ATV), Lancashire (Granada), Yorkshire (Yorkshire), South of England (Southern), Wales and the West of England (HTV), Central Scotland (Scottish), East of England (Anglia), North-East England (Tyne Tees), South-West England (Westward), Northern Ireland (Ulster), North-East Scotland (Grampian), the Borders and Isle of Man (Border) and Channel Islands (Channel).

BBC Television on the other hand was born and bred in London, and the capital has remained its headquarters for programme making and scheduling. Some 46 per cent of its programmes are made in London against 35 per cent elsewhere in the United Kingdom. Before 1962, offerings from outside London were sparse, but then the BBC began to provide extended local news magazines for viewers in Scotland, Wales and Northern Ireland. Even so, until 1970, it had only three English regional centres: Birmingham serving the Midlands, Bristol the West Country and Manchester the North. Then five more regional centres were established in Norwich, Leeds, Newcastle-upon-Tyne, Southampton and Plymouth. Plans to increase the number of regional centres have been held up by financial pressures.

News and current affairs programmes are the most important part of the regional output of both ITV and the BBC.

News magazines
On BBC1 the main spot for regional affairs is within the framework of the *Nationwide* programme, shown Monday to Friday from 6 pm. After the opening by Michael Barratt or Frank Bough the programme divides, each region having twenty-five minutes of local news and

Michael Barratt

current affairs under titles like *Look North* (in Newcastle), *Midlands Today* (Birmingham), *Points West* (Bristol) and *Scene Around Six* (Northern Ireland). Then the regions are reunited with London and their reporters contribute local angles and views on aspects of national issues. This formula enables local viewpoints and interests to gain a wider audience.

On ITV the regional programmes, shown at the same time, are separate, presented entirely by their individual link-men from studios in London, Birmingham, Manchester, Leeds, Glasgow, Edinburgh, Cardiff, Belfast, Southampton, Newcastle, Bristol, Norwich, Plymouth, Aberdeen, Carlisle, Dover and St Helier. The programmes, which have titles like *Report West*, *Westward Diary*, *About Anglia*, *Granada Reports* and *ATV Today*, usually open with from five to nine minutes of local news. Some of the bigger regions are subdivided for this purpose; for example, Southern Television's *Day by Day* presents simultaneously news for viewers in the east of its territory from its Dover studio and for viewers in the west from its Southampton studio. The news is followed by current affairs items.

The popularity of these regional programmes is shown by the frequency with which they get into the area top ten charts. They often achieve bigger audiences in their regions than do the national news

Eamonn Andrews interviews John Lennon and Yoko Ono for the London programme
Today

Southern Television cameraman filming a blaze at Fawley oil refinery

A regional cameraman takes to the air for a helicopter shot

programmes. *Day by Day* is permanently in the Southern area's top
ten, and half the adult population of the area watch it at least three
times a week. The range of local information programmes, in the early
evening and at other times, is considerable. Typically, Border
Television in Carlisle presents regularly *Border News and Lookaround*
from Monday to Friday, *Border Sports Review* (a Friday evening
preview of the week-end sport), *Border Diary* (concerned with forth-
coming events), *Border Month* (a look-back on news and events of the
past month with an invited audience putting questions), *Border
Parliamentary Report* (a monthly review of events at Westminster by
local MPs), *Border Forum* (after-dinner conversations between local
celebrities), *Border People and Places* (miscellaneous film documentaries) and *Police Call* (a weekly report on local crime in the region).
    Channel Television, with many French-speaking viewers, transmits
in French as well as English. Regular French language programmes
include *Bulletin Météorologique*, a daily weather forecast, *Actualités*, a
newscast four nights a week, and *Commentaires*, a weekly current
affairs programme. HTV, serving Wales and the West, transmits in
Welsh as well as English.
    A comparatively recent development in regional programmes has
been 'open access' television, in which programme time and technical
facilities are made available to outsiders to present a point of view.

Former office cleaner May Hobbs (centre) in an Open Door *programme produced by the Cleaners Action group*

BBC2 began transmitting such programmes nationally in 1973 under the title *Open Door*. A specially formed Community Programme Unit invited organizations to apply for forty minutes air-time and early programmes were on the Gypsy Council and the admission of women to the clergy. The format, which had already been pioneered in some ITV regions, is well suited to regional broadcasting and a number of regions have carried similar series. Typically the Tyne Tees *Access* series has provided a platform for the Durham Cyrenians (offering help for the homeless), the Hartlepool Ratepayers' Action Group, the Teesside Consumer Group, and local representatives of organizations such as Women in Need (concerned with battered wives), Save the Unborn Child (anti-abortion) and Gingerbread (one-parent families).

Regional facilities

Every region has its own specialities and long-running stories: in Ulster the political situation and the bombings; in the north-east of Scotland the search for North Sea oil; in East Anglia the fishing dispute with Iceland; in the South-West the battles for, and with, holidaymakers; in London the activities of the Greater London

Council. Stories like these occupy the time of film crews regularly, but in the regions crews have to be ready to switch between major stories and the parochial. A crew may cover an air crash or a murder like an ITN or BBC News crew. (The region may make its film available to the national news.) A crew may equally cover in the course of a day a sailing race, the topping-off of a civic centre and the growth of a mysterious plant in a council house garden. Editors have to concern themselves with other considerations in addition to the news value of stories. They aim to show the flag as far as possible in every corner of their territories and therefore, if there are two magazine-type stories of equal weight on the diary, a crew will probably be sent to the town which is less frequently in the news.

In the regions a film crew, by union agreement, commonly consists of two cameramen and a sound recordist. But staffing varies considerably. Channel Television, smallest of the ITV companies, serving a mere 107,000 viewers, has two news film units, one in Jersey and one in Guernsey, Anglia Television, serving 3·1 millions in the East of England, has four film units (two in Norwich and one each in King's Lynn and Luton). Yorkshire Television, one of the 'Big Five' ITV companies serving 5·4 millions, has eight film crews. All use, to a greater or lesser extent, freelance cameramen and reporters. Anglia, for example, has thirty attached cameramen and a hundred correspondents who telephone their copy to typists at the office. Freelance cameramen are often proprietors of local camera shops and usually their film is silent, requiring a voice-over commentary recorded in the studio. Resources are generally meagre compared with ITN and BBC Television News. At Westward Television the editor of the evening news bulletin has two sub-editors to assist him but has to write many of the stories himself. Communication problems are not concerned with the availability of satellites or the chartering of aircraft but with putting films on trains and deciding whether a cameraman can be spared to visit a village at the far end of the region.

'Getting film to the studio is probably the biggest problem for regional news programmes,' says Jim Wilson, once a reporter for an East Anglian daily newspaper, now Head of News at Anglia Television and responsible for the daily *About Anglia* programme. 'It is not nearly as easy as getting film to London. For example, trains run to London from all quarters, but in the country they tend to run north and south but not east and west, so we have to rely very heavily on despatch riders. Even then, if we want to interview someone in the extreme south of our area, it is usually easier to take him to London, interview him at ITN and send the interview down the line, than to bring him, or film of him, to Norwich.'

It is true that Yorkshire Television uses a helicopter for aerial filming and for moving newsmen to remote places, and that Southern Television, with its miles of coastline, owned a 72-feet long power vessel, *Southerner*, which was a floating outside broadcast unit. But a story that breaks in a remote part of a region in the afternoon is unlikely to make the bulletin in pictures that evening. It is doubtful, however, whether viewers are critical if the film is shown a day later.

The range and treatment of stories for a regional news programme were illustrated in the evidence presented to the Annan Committee on the Future of Broadcasting by the Independent Television Companies Association in 1975 with an account of a day in the newsroom of Tyne Tees Television at Newcastle. It began at 9.30 am:

> The editorial conference is in full swing. A thirty-minute news magazine is taking shape for 6 pm transmission. Journalists, film editors, production staff gather round the head of news, who is also producer. The news editor outlines the day: American-owned factory may close as orders fall; angry village fights planners on minerals exploration; local policeman's gallantry award for tackling armed man; gypsies evicted from forest site; school fire; computerized meals at new hospitals; beer shortage threatened as draymen strike; lorry driver trapped in crash.
>
> This news is for immediate coverage. Some cameramen have been on location since dawn. Also available on videotape: parents and schoolmasters debate English teaching methods; new uniforms for nurses (both video-recorded in studio the previous day).
>
> Producer, magazine editor, scriptwriters and sub-editors discuss story treatments. Reporters throw in ideas. Studio director and production assistant rough out a camera script, the master document from which everyone will work. A police tip-off interrupts the planning: £50,000 snatched from big store in morning raid. Reporter and camera crew are despatched. The day looks newsy, though a little heavy. In just over eight hours the right 'mix' must be provided to catch and hold viewer interest. Some lighter items are considered; a retired general running his own railway in his attic; an exhibition of electronic art which is baffling some citizens abroad . . .

The routine of the day is similar to that of a national television news organization, but there are differences in the basis of selection when the producer, with the editor, ponders the choice of item to open the programme: 'Store snatch or factory closure? News desk reports the factory interview very low-key; unions still hoping to avert total shutdown. The producer understands; he is part of the region too. Local jobs are more important than news stories.'

So the store snatch is put first, followed by the police award and the factory closure. A Common Market speech and the parent–teacher debate make mid-magazine offerings; eviction of the gypsies is slotted to enliven the second half. Shorter films and into-camera newsbriefs break up the longer items, with a story on nurses' uniforms providing an endpiece. At 5.40 the final camera moves and links are rehearsed in the studio.

'The producer, sitting behind the director, remains faintly unhappy with the top end of the running order. It will get by, but something is lacking. . . . Minutes later he takes the call which is to transform the day. The reporter on police award persuades him to follow the medal presentation film with a studio live spot featuring the whole family. As a camera-car brings them through rush-hour traffic, the producer takes a second, bolder decision – to lead on the story and run store snatch as number two. From control-room comes a series of brisk instructions: a camera is shifted, studio chairs rearranged, a new pro- gramme "intro" written, less urgent news film earmarked for cuts to avoid a programme overrun, the police award film run up to the telecine starting gate. As ITN's early bulletin signs off seconds before 6 pm the policeman, his wife and excited small daughter are seated in the studio with the reporter who will interview them. The family are a little breathless but totally engaging: modest local hero and articulate wife. It is also the little girl's birthday. After the film and live inter- views a cake is brought on glittering with hastily procured candles. She blows them out with a single puff to applause from the studio crew. At last the producer looks relaxed. The missing ingredient had been sheer human warmth.'

The regions constitute a training ground for the networked pro- grammes. For example, Ivor Mills of ITN and Julian Pettifer of *Panorama* were formerly with Southern Television's *Day by Day*. The regions recruit mainly from local newspapers, and reporters usually spend about a month writing scripts and voicing reports before being sent on the road. They learn fast in the regions because they are required to be performers rather than just reporters. The regions like to show their men participating, whether it is standing in for a Father Christmas at a local store or donning sou'wester and oilskins to go out with a lifeboat. A television reporter can soon become a celebrity in his area, though unknown to the rest of the country. But like all local journalists they have to live and work among the people on whom they report, compared to the national newsman who moves on after filing his story. And local reporters are not strangers to drama. In the Midlands a man facing eviction proceedings was upset by what he felt was an unfairly tough interview, so he returned to the studio armed with a shotgun in search of the reporter. He was dissuaded from using it by a priest who was there to deliver the close-down epilogue.

Chapter 12

Reporting wars

No longer are wars fought by forgotten armies in far-off countries. Television brings them into the drawing-room. No other medium can convey as dramatically and as immediately the acts of courage and of horror. And no one is in greater danger in war than a television team, particularly its cameraman. Sometimes he runs greater risks than the warring parties because, if he is to do his job properly, he cannot keep his head down; he will be exposed to fire while soldiers take cover. Cameramen admit that watching the action through their viewfinders gives them a sense of detachment and distances them from reality; they are so involved in doing their job that they are unaware of the danger at the time. Only this detachment or an incredible stubbornness can explain the conduct of Leonardo Henricsson, a cameraman who, in Chile in 1973, pointed his lens at the National Guard and had a rifle pointed at him in return. He carried on filming, ignoring two shots fired at him. A third shot killed him. The film he took survived and has been shown on television. He literally recorded his own execution.

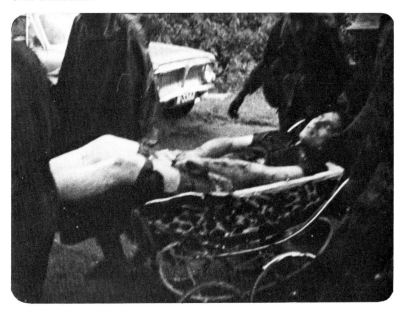

Viewers saw wounded Peter Sissons wheeled from an ambush like this

Students stone Russian tanks in Czechoslovakia

British television has had its casualties. Ted Stoddart, a BBC sound recordist, was killed when he trod on a mine in Cyprus in 1974. Martin Fletcher, a Visnews agency cameraman, was slightly injured himself but filmed the subsequent events. As did ITN's Cyril Page when his reporter colleague, Peter Sissons, was shot in both legs by a sniper in Biafra in 1968. Yet television newsmen are never *ordered* to go to a war. It is not necessary; there are always sufficient volunteers, even though war has rarely been absent from bulletins in recent years.

The importance that war has for television is matched by the importance that television has assumed for the military. They regard it, and seek to use it, as part of their propaganda effort, to gain sympathy for their cause and viewpoint. 'War's no good today unless you can show it,' was the cynical way in which a veteran war correspondent summed up the military attitude.

Facilities

Television men strive to be objective, but if anyone doubts the degree to which television news can influence opinion it is only necessary to recall Czechoslovakia in 1968 when Russian T55 tanks clattered into Prague to end Alexander Dubček's liberalization. The Czech television service sent outside broadcast vans into the streets and transmitted live. The pictures were monitored by Austrian television, videotaped and relayed over the European Broadcasting Union network to Britain and the rest of Europe. They were also retransmitted by satellite to the United States and other parts of the world. And so, in every free country, viewers saw bold Czech students shouting defiance at the Red Army and daubing their tanks with 'Go home' messages. When the Russians belatedly shut down the Czech television stations a wounded cameraman managed to smuggle film out to Austria.

The world was impotent to intervene in Prague but it expressed its abhorrence of the Russian action by demonstrations outside Soviet embassies. The Russians were left in no doubt about the disgust they had aroused and Dubček, who had been arrested, was at least returned alive from Moscow. With this kind of reaction possible, most armies, including Britain's, now have officers whose function is to provide facilities for television crews to cover their activities – or at any rate those they want covered – and television executives have visited the Staff College to lecture on television's needs. Basically, these are facilities to reach the battleground, to record impressions of it and to present them quickly to the public. They are the same requirements that William Howard Russell had when he was covering the Crimean war for *The Times* more than a century ago, but then despatches took a long while to reach London and readers' conclusions depended entirely upon his words. Today television brings war into every living-room for viewers to see with their own eyes.

The extent of the facilities afforded varies between armies. All correspondents agree that the US Army is the most open. 'In Vietnam you had only to get your accreditation and you could visit any firebase you liked,' says John Pilger, the Australian reporter who covered the war for *World in Action* and his own series, *Pilger*, as well as for the *Daily Mirror*. 'I still can't quite believe that wars are really like Vietnam.' At the other end of the scale was Biafra where 'There were no facilities beyond a lift in a Red Cross plane'. In the Middle East Israel gave more ready access to the fighting arena than the Egyptians, though they in turn were more television-minded than the Syrians. This was obvious from the coverage, and subsequently the Arab League held a conference in Cairo to discuss their handling of the medium and the lessons to be learned.

British Army officers appearing in television news programmes are invariably assured and articulate. Some of them appear to be television 'naturals'. In fact, all British Army officers are now trained to appear on television. The army has closed-circuit television coaching facilities at the Royal Military Academy at Sandhurst, the Staff College at Camberley, the Army School of Education at Beaconsfield and elsewhere. And whenever a regiment is being posted to Northern Ireland it is visited by a mobile television unit and coaching is given to all the officers and at least some of the NCOs. Viewers never see officers with unattractive television personalities. Television entered the army's training schedules late in 1969 as a result of experience in

Hooded members of an Ulster paramilitary force posing for World in Action

Ulster. 'When something happened involving the army there were always five women and four priests to give their account of what happened,' remarks a senior officer at the Ministry of Defence. 'We had to be able to put up our own spokesmen, and the finest spokesman is the chap who was on the spot.'

British armed forces are generally reckoned to be co-operative, though not as open as their American counterparts. Pilger says: 'In Vietnam you could walk into any mess, you could talk to anyone, but you can't get right in among the British Army in Northern Ireland in the same way.' Christopher Wain, defence correspondent of the BBC and formerly of ITN, agrees. 'Despite the army's television training, it can take time to set up a TV interview,' he says. 'Newspapermen can chat to a commanding officer without difficulty, but if the matter is sensitive a request for an interview on film will be referred to Northern Ireland army headquarters at Lisburn, from where it may be referred to the Ministry of Defence in London, who may refer it to a minister, and then the army will want advance notice of the questions to be asked, by which time the newspapermen will have done their job and moved on.' This is in strong contrast to the American open-access creed in Vietnam. The nightly television coverage sickened the American public of the war, and there is no doubt that this had a significant effect upon the administration and the ultimate course it took, irrespective of the rights and wrongs of US involvement.

Censorship

Before that point was reached the US Army's openness had caused it a number of embarrassments. Whichever side they portray in a conflict, the television cameras may be relied on to reveal bravery and hardship. They will show the effects of the enemy's actions such as bomb-devastated hospitals, and they will show victims of the enemy's cruelty. ('Anyone here speak English and been raped?' was the alleged cry of one television correspondent in the Congo on entering newly freed areas.) But the cameras will also record any brutal acts by the army they accompany. In 1965 the CBS network filmed US Marines setting fire to Vietnamese dwellings in the village of Cam Ne with cigarette lighters. Morley Safer, a Canadian reporter, alleged that 150 homes were burned in reprisal for a burst of gunfire. American headquarters in Saigon retorted, 'Marines do not burn houses or villages unless they are fortified', and claimed that no more than fifty houses were destroyed and that the Marines had previously suffered heavy fire. The Pentagon virtually accused the network of treason and a Marine colonel told Safer that he would not be responsible for what his men might do to him if he accompanied them on another mission. (In fact Safer did, and reported on it.)

In 1969 CBS came under Pentagon fire again for the persistence of its investigations into the My Lai massacre a year and a half earlier. Yet in 1970 John Pilger was able to make an award-winning *World in Action* programme called *The Grunts at Snuffy*. The Grunts were eighteen-year-old national servicemen and Snuffy was a Vietnam outpost. His film showed servicemen talking about their pot-smoking and 'fragging', the killing or maiming of unpopular officers, and exposed the disintegration of US Army morale. Pilger says that there was no attempt to stop him filming, though he thinks it might have been more difficult had he been representing an American network rather than a foreign one. For governments feel that their country's television men owe loyalty on a 'My country, right or wrong' basis. Dean Rusk demanded of American television men on one occasion, 'The question is, whose side are you on? I'm the Secretary of State and I'm on our side.' He echoed Sir Anthony Eden who, having launched the Suez operation as premier in 1956, felt the World War II 'us against them' attitude should prevail and objected unsuccessfully to television granting equal time to the Leader of the Opposition to speak against his action. Similarly, when television presents interviews with both army and IRA spokesmen in Northern Ireland, some people feel it is granting equal time to Jesus and Judas.

Guerrillas in Portuguese East Africa seen in another World in Action *programme*

Yet formal censorship of television in the sense of vetting film is rare today. ITN's first war was Suez, during which Robin Day was seen emerging from a manhole surrounded by tanks (after conducting an interview below the road) to sign off with the words 'From the sewers of Port Said I return you to the studios of ITN'. In the early stages of the campaign television film had to be pooled and was censored at the War Office before release, but that lasted only a few days. Israeli censors viewed television film during the 1973 Yom Kippur war, but obligingly allowed it to be run at high speed.

Of course, correspondents have to refrain from disclosing military secrets in their commentaries, but the commonest form of censorship today is simply refusing facilities for television crews to get to the fighting, which is effective enough. Subtle hindrances can also be imposed. Chris Wain says that in Mozambique in 1973 taxis could become suddenly unavailable to television men, phone-calls could become disconnected and films could go missing in transit. But in Vietnam there was no censorship. Lyndon Johnson said later: 'I believe I was the only president in this country who presided over a war in which there was no censorship of news despatches. The effect of bringing Vietnam and all its travail to the evening news screen will not be known, I believe, for a long time. Showing the suffering and the savage combat with an elusive enemy was the price we paid for a free press. It was a price worth paying, all things considered, but it was still a heavy price for the nation.'

The public as well as governments have criticized television war coverage. 'Too much blood,' say some. Certainly news is the most violent segment of television. A BBC audience research report in 1972, containing an analysis of all three channels in the London area over a six-month period, calculated that the news programmes had screened 10·4 violent incidents per hour compared with only two in drama programmes and even less in others. One of the ghastliest incidents ever shown was when South Vietnam's Brigadier-General Nguyen Ngoc Loan was seen to walk up to a captured Vietcong officer and cold-bloodedly shoot him through the head. Recognition of such facts of life and death is affirmed in ITV's Code on Violence: 'Violence has always been, and still is, widespread throughout the world, so violent scenes in news and current affairs are inevitable.' And yet it has been suggested that television can beautify war, in that a napalm fireball, which is a horrifying and terrible thing, can look pretty in colour. Some viewers fear that the presence of television cameras may precipitate events in war as they have at demonstrations where a television company's question, 'What time does the demonstration begin?' has been met with the answer, 'What time can you be there?'

In Nigeria in 1968 General Gowon, the Federal Commander, was accused of allowing his subordinates to slaughter Biafran officers. To show that he did not condone this he invited television cameramen to film the execution of one of his officers found guilty of such conduct. The officer was shown being led out, blindfolded and tied to a stake. What was not shown was the interruption of a cameraman yelling 'Hold it!' while he adjusted his camera. Whether the execution would have taken place without an audience must be a matter for conjecture. Cameras can only record what happened and journalists can only give their interpretation of events.

A complaint voiced by the Pentagon in the Vietnam war was that, by following small units, television showed only a 'sampling' of the action rather than the big picture, but every soldier knows that it is the small unit which sees the action, and that war always looks better at army headquarters than it does from a foxhole.

Certainly the presence of television cameras in the fighting zones has reduced the amount of imaginative and purple prose by newspaper writers. Television men claim that they 'don't meet a lot of newspaper-men at the sharp end of a war'. This is not a charge that can be levied against television crews. The public sees what they see; they have to get in among it. And it is dangerous. But television units are always striving to get to the action faster. When two companies of the Parachute Regiment were despatched to subdue the allegedly rebellious populace of Anguilla in the West Indies in 1969 the first boat to hit the beach was one holding an ITN crew. On that occasion the troops charged ashore to be greeted by amused, puzzled and unarmed islanders, but when Turkish paratroops dropped in Cyprus in 1974 ITN's Michael Nicholson was there to greet and interview them, while fields were ablaze from explosions and villagers fled to their dug-outs.

Television men are also seeking to get their reports back faster and the day of instant war grows nearer. In Vietnam they could breakfast, go out and shoot pictures of the war and, thanks to satellite communications and time differences, have their pictures on *News at Ten* the same night. Packed in plastic bags the films were flown from Saigon to Hong Kong where they were processed and 'birded' (transmitted by satellite) to Madrid and passed on to London by land-line. Some American crews are already equipped with hand-held video cameras and back-pack videotape machines, because videotape can be played back immediately without processing. The day is coming when all wars will be shot by cameras using videotape recording rather than film cameras. This will make live coverage of war, already possible, more practicable.

The thought of war shown live on television, with someone's husband, someone's father, someone's son dying before viewers' eyes is horrifying. But it will come – unless James Hagerty, the former Press Secretary to President Eisenhower, later a television executive, was right when he said of the Vietnam coverage: 'By showing war in its stinking reality we have taken away the glory and have shown that negotiation is the only way to solve international problems.'

Michael Nicholson heads his ITN film crew in Vietnam

Chapter 13

Reporting politics

Politics and politicians provide a considerable proportion of news and current affairs stories and both the BBC and ITN have office space in the House of Commons for their political staffs. The BBC, as the longer established and bigger organization with radio as well as television programmes, has a room of its own, while ITN shares accommodation with newspapermen.

The ITN team numbers three: Julian Haviland, the political editor, and two correspondents. But working closely with them from the same desk are three other correspondents, one for Thames Television, one for Granada and one representing the other ITV companies. Between them they have to be available to provide information and interpretation seven days a week, for even at week-ends there are political speeches in the constituencies, but television can allow little time for these, as bulletins are shorter and sport has to be included. The busiest day of the week is Thursday, when the Prime Minister answers questions, the Cabinet meets, the Leader of the House announces the business for the following week (which gives MPs the opportunity to initiate mini-debates on a variety of subjects under the guise of questions) and back-benchers of both parties hold meetings to discuss tactics.

The political editor's day

Haviland's day begins at 7 or 8 am when he listens to the radio news, reads the morning papers, warns the news desk of any possible stories which he had not foreseen the previous day, and may answer calls from the office asking advice about getting an MP to appear in the lunch-time news programme. He gets to the House at about 11 am and goes to the ITN desk close by the Press Gallery, from which correspondents can watch debates in the Chamber. It is in an area provided with its own restaurant, bar and reference library and a closed-circuit television system that will display the name of the member speaking in the Chamber, the subject of the debate and give an audible warning when there is to be a vote.

His first job is to read through *Hansard* for the previous day and the Order Paper for the current one, looking for any stories or leads to stories that may be concealed there. If he has time he may then look in on one of the committee meetings where the real work of legislation is done and where the details of a bill may be considerably amended. He may go into the lobby to talk to MPs as they leave the committee rooms for lunch before going to lunch himself, with a minister, an opposition front-bencher, a government information spokesman or a back-bench MP. Haviland says: 'A lot of back-bench MPs are very good reporters. They beaver away finding out what is going on and you get to know which back-bench MP specializes in which particular field of policy and which knows, for instance, about Home Office affairs and is likely to be able to tell you if someone is going to be let out of jail on parole.'

After lunch comes question-time in the House. The political editor may attend it or he may go into the lobbies to intercept MPs coming and going from the Chamber. On most days there will also be parliamentary or government papers to be collected and read, any of which may contain an important story, possibly concealed in the small print. At 3.30 he will certainly be in the Chamber for the end of question-time, because between then and the start of the main debate is the time when anything out of the way will occur. If the Prime Minister has a major decision to announce, a minister is to make a statement about a disaster or an MP is to ask whether a newspaper article constitutes a breach of privilege, this is when it will happen. The main debate follows, and again the political reporters will be torn between listening to the debate and working in the lobbies, but experience helps them to predict when newsworthy passages are likely to occur. The BBC has gallery correspondents to cover debates and lobby correspondents, who then interpret the significance and fill in the background story from private talks with ministers and members. ITN staff combine both functions. 'We are hybrids,' says Haviland. Originally ITN men doubled the jobs because of restrictions on the number of people the company was allowed in the overcrowded House, but now they prefer to work this way.

A debate usually reaches its climax at about 10 pm and the last speech comes between 9.30 and 10 pm. Normally the House divides for a vote at 10 pm and the result will be known about fifteen minutes later, though sometimes there are two votes, a vote on an opposition amendment first and then a vote on the main motion, so the outcome will be known just before *News at Ten* goes off the air. This timing gives ITN's 10 pm news an advantage over the BBC1's 9 pm bulletin though, until 1976, the BBC had a useful advantage over ITN in being the only one to have a Westminster studio. The BBC studio until 1976 was in College Mews, set into a wall near Westminster Abbey and only five minutes' walk from the Press Gallery.

Until 1976, although ITN had a direct-line telephone from its desk at the Press Gallery so that a correspondent's voice could be fed into a bulletin, its nearest studio was at ITN headquarters in Wells Street. This meant a taxi journey and, to reach the studio in time to appear in the 5.50 pm news bulletin, the correspondent had to allow about forty-five minutes because of the rush-hour traffic. To get to the studio for *News at Ten*, he had to leave before the result of a vote was known. In both cases he would be nervous at being out of touch with the House where a story can break unexpectedly at any time. So ITN made much use of its outside broadcast unit for political news, setting up behind the railings of Westminster Abbey opposite the St Stephen's entrance to the House, the entrance used by the public. This meant that the correspondent could be on the screen five minutes after leaving the gallery. However, since April 1976, ITN has had its own parliamentary studio operational in the former New Scotland Yard, the Norman Shaw building, which now provides office accommodation for MPs. The studio now also serves the regional ITV companies who frequently want to interview MPs from their areas on matters of purely local interest and, since all the main regional programmes begin at 6 pm, there is a great need for studio facilities at that time. MPs are as reluctant as reporters to leave the House for any length of time and are much more ready to undertake a short walk than a car ride across the West End. The BBC's Westminster studio is now located next door to ITN's. Both have their lighting and cameras remotely controlled from the main studios.

Debates and elections
With the extensive coverage given to political affairs on television today it is hard to credit that in 1955 it was forbidden to broadcast on television controversial material about subjects due to be discussed in Parliament during the following fortnight. The BBC had observed for a long time on television and radio an agreement with the main parties not to anticipate parliamentary debates. This was no great concern to television when it was primarily a medium of entertainment, but in 1955, the year that ITV began in London, the ban was enforced on both organizations by a formal notice from the government.

The television companies fought the so-called Fourteen Day Rule on two counts. The first was that it was undemocratic. Newspapers were free to discuss, and express opinions on, matters of public concern, and although television editorializing is forbidden, there seemed no good reason why television journalists should be prevented from broadcasting balanced views until after Parliament had decided an issue and it was too late for public opinion to make itself heard. The second was that the rule was unworkable because it was not always known fourteen days in advance what Parliament might debate.

After an investigation by a select committee, in December 1956 the Postmaster-General revoked the Fourteen Day Rule. Soon television journalists began to look at the coverage of general elections. Until this time, apart from transmitting party election broadcasts, the BBC closed down political discussion as soon as an election campaign began, depriving electors of information when their interest waxed keenest. This was because the Representation of the People Act of 1949 imposed restrictions on expenses that could be incurred in 'promoting or procuring the election of a candidate' and it was feared that a television programme might be held to infringe the Act.

The breakthrough came in February 1958 at a by-election at Rochdale. The BBC announced: 'We do not intend to depart from our usual practice in by-elections that we do not influence voters, nor report the campaigns in news bulletins.' But ITV was now in being in Lancashire, and Granada Television, whose area included Rochdale, had other ideas. After consulting eminent lawyers about the Representation of the People Act and the Television Act of 1954, which obliged it to observe 'due impartiality' on political matters, it decided to allot equal studio time to each of the three candidates, to interview voters in the streets and to show outside broadcasts of the vote counting and the declaration of the results. Democracy survived undamaged and so the general election of 1959 was covered by both ITV and the BBC more thoroughly than ever before.

Granada introduced *Marathon*, an election special in which all the parliamentary candidates from every constituency in its area were invited to appear and address the electors. More than two hundred candidates took part, so viewers saw their local candidates rather than just the party leaders on screen. Granada also transmitted *Fast Focus*, nine five-minute programmes in which people discussed issues arising from the parties' election broadcasts, *How an Election Works*, two programmes in which Bernard Braden investigated the mechanics of the electoral system, and *The Last Debate*, an eve-of-poll discussion by three candidates before an audience of three hundred.

Thus the foundations were laid for the massive coverage given to general elections today. Election night programmes are the biggest scheduled events in the television news calendar. Each news organization will employ some five hundred correspondents to telephone constituency results (and offer them inducements to beat the opposition). It will deploy more than twenty outside broadcast units and reporters in key constituencies. In the studio it will have as many as 150 people, from an anchor-man reading the results and reporting the news to panels of prominent politicians and trade unionists. All the skill of the graphics department will be brought to bear on ingenious visual displays, and caption-titling machines and computers will be brought into service. To a certain extent it could be said that television has taken over general elections and made them into television shows.

Robin Day interviews Lord Hailsham in a 1964 general election programme

Crowds in Trafalgar Square await the October 1974 election results on large-screen television

Early attempts by the BBC to add an extra dimension to television coverage of the results involved David Butler, a political economist, working out percentage 'swings' with a slide-rule and Robert McKenzie, a professor of sociology, illustrating these shifts in voting with a 'swingometer'. Then lightning-fast computers were enlisted, predicting the outcome of the election as soon as the first result was in, and updating the forecast through the night as more figures arrived. In the general elections of 1974 ITN linked its computer to a machine normally used for planning knitting patterns, modified to print out results in instant-picture form.

Television also makes much use of opinion polls on voters' intentions and at one time the BBC extended this feature by conducting a mini-poll in selected constituencies, asking voters leaving the booths how they voted, thus producing the most up-to-date possible forecast of the result before the official count. Julian Haviland says: 'A general election is one area of the political process where television has all the cards. It is allowed there, and people want to know the answer quickly. All the evidence is that people are interested to a very high degree. On average, 75 per cent of electors vote and, as it is wholly a voluntary act, that is an extraordinarily high level for three out of four to turn out. So people like to watch the results and they like comment on the results.'

However, it was felt widely that television overdid its coverage of the campaign in February 1974. BBC1 presented news and current affairs from 9 to 10 pm every night, more than half of which time was devoted to the campaign. At 10 pm came a party election broadcast. Popular series like *Colditz* and *The Liver Birds* had to be moved to make way for these programmes. And, of course, current affairs series like *Panorama* and *The Money Programme* also covered election issues. The BBC's audience research showed later that a substantial majority of viewers had found the coverage excessive. There was also criticism of the form of the coverage; two-thirds of the respondents felt that too much attention had been concentrated on the party leaders. But the most interesting question – whether the coverage had swayed people's minds in deciding how to vote – remained unanswered. The evidence was insufficient, said the BBC.

For the October 1974 election coverage was throttled back a little and protests were fewer.

Party politicals

Almost certainly the party political broadcast is the least popular part of television. The first agreement on these programmes was signed by the BBC in 1947, and by tradition the BBC still provides the producer and studio facilities for them, though content and presentation is for the party concerned. Every year a certain amount of broadcasting time is offered to the main parties, who then decide on its allocation between themselves in proportion to their vote at the last general election. It amounts to about fifteen broadcasts totalling nearly two and a half hours, but extra broadcasts are arranged during the campaigning period preceding a general election, when any party nominating fifty or more candidates on a national basis qualifies for time. At the October 1974 election the Conservative and Labour parties each had five programmes of ten minutes duration; the Liberals had four programmes of ten minutes each, and the National Front had one of five minutes. In Scotland the Scottish Nationalists had two broadcasts of ten minutes each, and in Wales the Welsh Nationalists had one of ten minutes. As the Communist Party fielded less than fifty candidates it got none, which led it to claim sourly but accurately that anyone with the money for fifty deposits could buy time on television.

The presentation of party politicals varies. The Conservatives once used professional film-makers like Bryan Forbes to put a gloss on their programmes, but the reaction was that the products were *too* slick. By contrast the Liberals produced four programmes for a total of £100 in 1974. Many viewers find them all objectionable, the worst feature being that they are shown on at least two channels simultaneously. This has obtained since 1956. Viewers also object to the use of peak-hour viewing-time for the presentation of a one-sided picture and the slanging of opponents, for current affairs programmes have accustomed viewers to seeing politicians' views challenged.

A BBC audience survey after the February 1974 election showed that, of five different ways of presenting the campaign, 'questions put to politicians' was deemed the most interesting and 'reporters' comments' on the election the most informative, while party election broadcasts came last on both counts, even though the programmes were viewed on average by 21 per cent of the population – about $10\frac{1}{2}$ million people. However, politicians of all parties put a high value on the continuance of party politicals as the only form of broadcast wholly under their control, and resist criticism of the genre.

Politicians on television

Television's importance to politicians was demonstrated dramatically in the United States in 1952 when Richard M. Nixon was a candidate for the vice-presidency alongside General Eisenhower for the presidency. When rumours spread of a secret Nixon fund, he bought television time at a cost of $75,000 (subscribed by supporters) to make what has become known as the 'Checkers speech', a classic example of vote-winning schmaltz. He began, candidly:

'My fellow Americans, I come before you tonight as a candidate for the vice-presidency and as a man whose honesty and integrity has been questioned.'

He explained the fund and defended it, and went on:

'One other thing I probably should tell you, because if I don't they will probably be saying this about me too. We did get something, a gift, after the nomination. A man down in Texas heard Pat on the radio mention the fact that our two youngsters would like to have a dog and, believe it or not, the day before we left on this campaign trip we got a message from Union station in Baltimore saying they had a package for us. We went down to get it. You know what it was? It was a little cocker spaniel dog in a crate that he had sent all the way from Texas – black and white, spotted, and our little girl Tricia, the six-year-old, named it Checkers. And you know, the kids, like all kids, loved the dog and I just want to say this, right now, that regardless of what they say about it, we are going to keep it.'

The show-business paper *Variety*, reviewing it as a programme, called it 'a brilliant feat in political journalism', and Nixon duly became Vice-President.

But in 1960 Nixon fell victim to television when he took on John F. Kennedy, his opponent for the presidency, in a series of four television debates. Eisenhower warned Nixon: 'Don't build him up by appearing with him on TV.' But Nixon did and his image was considered less appealing than Kennedy's, partly because of his tendency to 5 o'clock shadow and to perspire. Kennedy won the presidency and declared: 'It was TV more than anything that turned the tide.' Nixon worked hard at his television technique before his next – and successful – nomination.

It was argued similarly in Britain that Harold Wilson was a master of television, while Sir Alec Douglas-Home appeared unhappy on it. Edward Heath's television image was also compared unfavourably with Wilson's. All the main parties have studio facilities to coach their members to appear at their best on television but in the end it seems that some politicians naturally screen well and others do not. Those who do, and are sought after by television, are not necessarily ministers or ex-ministers. Cyril Smith, the heavyweight Liberal MP, disclosed to his constituents in 1974 that he had earned £1,500 in television fees, and the 'appearance money' paid by current affairs programmes is not extravagant.

The selection of MPs to appear on television is watched closely by party leaders and officials. At one time television tried to observe a balance within every controversial programme, having equal numbers of speakers for each viewpoint and allowing them exactly the same amount of time. Programmes were so balanced that opposing opinions cancelled each other out, and, based on what he had seen, a

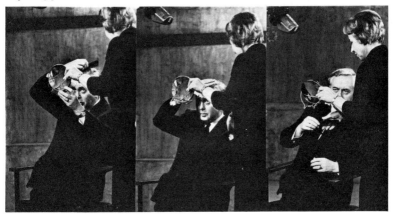

Harold Wilson grooms himself for a programme on The Power of a Prime Minister

viewer could hardly reach any conclusion. The effect was stultifying. This balancing act was carried to extraordinary lengths. Any appearance by an MP, even if it was in a programme about Mahler or antique snuff-boxes where his political affiliations had no more relevance than his choice of tailor, was still logged as an appearance for his party and an MP from the other side would have to be featured in another programme to redress the balance. Even so, the television companies found it was not sufficient merely to balance appearances by Conservatives against appearances by Labour; they were expected to take account not only of differences between parties but within parties.

The issue came to a head in the fifties over a BBC discussion programme called *In the News.* The regular panel of knockabout controversialists consisted of two left-wingers, Michael Foot and A. J. P. Taylor, and two right-wingers, Lord Boothby and W. J. Brown. Conservative and Labour Party executives objected that they did not always represent official party politics and thinking; they wanted orthodox party men substituted. Rather than hand over the programme to the parties, the BBC eventually dropped the show, whereupon the newborn ITV took it over with the same four protagonists under the apt title *Free Speech.* Later ITN developed a weekly series of thirteen-minute interviews called *Tell the People* in which, apart from film stars, it featured Macmillan and Gaitskell, Butler and Benn, and broke all the old rules of balance in that there was no opposing speaker within the single programme.

Today it is accepted that, while the companies must balance different points of view, it is not necessary to do this within one programme. The balance may be achieved over a period, often within a series of related programmes. Problems of balance remain, however, particularly at election times, for a candidate may be guilty of illegal practice under the Representation of the People Act if he takes part in a broadcast about his constituency when a rival candidate declines to do so and will not agree to the broadcast being made without him. Party chiefs are quick to claim unfairness in balance. Lord Hill of Luton, former Chairman of the BBC, recalled several instances in his book *Behind the Screen*, published in 1974.

When Harold Wilson as Prime Minister and Edward Heath as Leader of the Opposition made speeches one week-end in 1970 the BBC sent a film crew to Heath's meeting but used a still picture of Wilson. The Government Chief Whip demanded details of the time devoted to each and a transcript. At the time of the 1970 election *Panorama* sought the Foreign Secretary, Michael Stewart, to appear in a programme. Wilson wanted Denis Healey on defence instead. In the meantime the BBC had booked Sir Alec Douglas-Home for the Conservatives and Home did not want to discuss defence with Healey. In the end they did separate pieces from different parts of the country: 'It was not a great success,' wrote Hill.

On the eve of poll in 1970 the BBC News broadcast a piece of film with Heath warning that devaluation would follow a Labour victory and a longer piece by James Callaghan replying. Harold Wilson telephoned complaining that Callaghan did not balance the Leader of the Opposition and threatened not to allow the BBC facilities in his Huyton constituency on election night.

Television and politicians live in uneasy coexistence, needing yet suspicious of each other. Periodically there are major rows. In 1971 there was a squabble over a BBC programme called *Yesterday's Men*, about Labour front-benchers who had lost office in 1970. Politicians complained about the whole style of the programme, but the real storm was over questions David Dimbleby put to Harold Wilson asking how much he had earned from the publication of his memoirs. Wilson stopped the interview, called for the Director-General and demanded that this part of the interview be scrapped. The programme was shown without it, but an anonymous telephone caller leaked the offending questions and answers to the press.

In 1972 there was a more important disagreement when BBC1 announced a programme entitled *The Question of Ulster – an Enquiry into the Future*. The BBC had invited Lord Devlin to chair it and representatives of various factions (though not the IRA) to take part. Reginald Maudling, the Home Secretary, held that such a programme would be irresponsible and inflammatory, but the BBC claimed the same freedom to discuss Ulster as the press. The broadcast went out,

Ludovic Kennedy introduces the BBC's criticized examination of the Ulster troubles

and though certainly responsible it was widely considered to be dull.

Brian Young, Director-General of the IBA, has summed up the TV–Westminster relationship in these words:

'The view of British governments has always been that television is free to criticize, to comment and to probe, provided that this is done fairly and with a real awareness of both sides of the question. It must be impartial rather than partisan, since it holds a monopoly position, but governments have always recognized that television must be free to challenge an official line as well as to support such a line. So a democracy needs broadcasting services which are not run by government and this has always been accepted. . . . Members of Parliament believe that as elected representatives their views on all matters should carry weight and so they do. But if they were allowed to carry over-riding weight, then the way would be open for general political control over broadcasting.'

Televising Parliament

One area in which television has met continued resistance from politicians is over facilities to screen parliamentary proceedings. In many countries of Western Europe television's right of access to Parliament is taken for granted, but the House of Commons has turned down proposals for experimental television coverage of its proceedings four times in nine years. The objections have been various. That television lights would grill members on their benches (though the companies say that the latest cameras require little extra lighting). That television would destroy the intimate atmosphere of the House (to which television men retort that MPs are not elected to enjoy club life). That to show proceedings in the Chamber when members are busy in committee rooms would give the impression that they play truant from debates (to which journalists reply that no one would want to screen routine proceedings). That television could not be trusted to edit proceedings honestly and fairly (though there have been few complaints about the summaries of debates given on television and radio). That members would be encouraged by the presence of cameras to play to the gallery. (But television has been

Cameramen film Chancellor Anthony Barber leaving Downing Street to present the 1972 Budget

covering the annual conferences of the three main parties and the TUC live since Granada first did so in 1962, without adverse results.)

What the television companies want is the right to install cameras in the House of Commons and to plug into the proceedings at any time, either to transmit them live or to record them for transmission later. Obviously, only major events like Budget Day would receive live coverage; most proceedings would be edited for use in news bulletins and special parliamentary programmes. However, MPs rejected proposals for an experiment with television by one vote in 1966, by twenty-six votes in 1972, by twenty-five votes in 1974 and twelve votes in 1975. One Labour MP greeted the 1975 result with a two-finger salute at the Press Gallery, but Phillip Whitehead, Labour MP and former producer of *This Week*, described it as 'one more example of the clubby side of the House of Commons overcoming reality'.

Voting has been free from party whips, with the result that in 1975 Harold Wilson voted for television, while his Agricultural Minister, Fred Peart, voted against it. The Leader of the Opposition, Margaret Thatcher, voted against, while her deputy, William Whitelaw, voted in favour. However, the House permitted experimental radio coverage for four weeks in 1975 by a majority of 172, and it seems inevitable that the right to show proceedings on television will come one day.

Chapter 14
Problems and pressures

It is estimated that 75 per cent of the public get most of their information from television. *News at Ten* and the *Nine O'Clock News* are each viewed by between 8 and 15 million nightly, and these television bulletins have an impact that the printed word seldom equals. As the US television newsman Walter Cronkite put it: 'You can pass by a headline, even if dramatic, but you cannot close your eyes to a dramatic picture that appears on TV.' Consequently, television news and current affairs are subjected to a close and continuing scrutiny by the thinking public, by leaders of opinion and particularly by newspapers, whose declining circulations reflect, in some part at least, the growth of television journalism.

Some criticisms that are levelled at television news inevitably concern matters of personal opinion and taste on which views will differ. There are still those who feel that the BBC's news is more 'official' than other forms, that items about the royal family should be given precedence and that sensational stories like that of the runaway MP John Stonehouse should not be given time at all. This recalls an attitude which the BBC abandoned two decades ago. There are also those who, as the BBC recorded in its annual report of 1974, accuse television news of 'harping on disaster and helping to create an atmosphere of gloom in the public mind'. Some of them feel that broadcasters 'should deliberately emphasize cheerful news'. The BBC pointed out that tragedy has always provided much of the raw material of news, that there are many news items that are 'good' or 'bad' according to different viewpoints, and that when there is 'happy' news that is newsworthy it is reported – because it is news and not because it is good or bad.

Charges like these are levelled just as frequently at newspapers, but one peculiar to television is that it has sometimes shown dramatic action film at the expense of important but less pictorial subjects. There is some truth in this but, since television news came of age, it happens less often. Nigel Ryan, Editor of ITN, says:

'In the early days television was tremendously anxious to prove that it could bring in pictures from foreign countries. Now that we know, and our public know, that we can get pictures from a battle-front in Cambodia the same day by satellite, we don't necessarily do it, unless it is going to bring in the most important information. We are far more confident of being able to keep our audience by applying strict news values.

Tragedy – television covers a disaster on the London Underground

'Always, obviously, there is the factor that television is to do with pictures, and when we have got pictures, there is a perfectly respectable temptation to use them, but in consciously being prepared to report the issues of inflation and the Common Market, we sacrifice pictures and take a risk on the audience. However, we discovered in the summer of 1972 when Peter Snow did a series of explanatory pieces about the Common Market, which we consciously decided to do at the expense of pictures and at the risk of boring our audience, that we did not lose any viewers.'

It is of course one of the problems of television news and current affairs programmes that they have to cater for readers of *The Times* and the *Sun* at the same time. There have been surveys showing that many viewers thought that EEC stood for Eastern Electricity Council or a chemical for killing flies, and that the Pentagon was the home of the American president or a mystical symbol, though in the context of stories about the Common Market or America's defence, as they would be mentioned in programmes, it is probable that they would have been understood. Nigel Ryan says:

'The whole craft of television news is presenting important information in a comprehensible manner. If we fail in being comprehended then we fail as a news service. We try not to use long words that people will not understand, but we are not an adult education class and if we started to patronize our viewers we would certainly lose them. We will publish something that we know is going to be over the heads of some of our audience, but we have to balance that against the need to reach a mass audience.

'We are a popular form of journalism. It is our business to remain popular in the sense that we wish to communicate with a large number of people. We do not intend to go "down market" and we do not need to do so. By remaining exactly where we are we reach a vast number of people and we put across a vast amount of serious information. That is the intellectual challenge and that is the satisfaction. It works.'

Trial by television

Perhaps the first serious criticism of television journalists in the fifties was for persistent questioning of statesmen and politicians. It led to complaints that television was, intervening in, or influencing, events. When John Freeman interviewed Frank Foulkes, Communist president of the Electrical Trades Union, in a *Panorama* programme, there was criticism in Parliament and the press. Lord Alexander of Hillsborough objected to people being interviewed as if they were 'prisoners in the dock and considered to be guilty before any trial'. A *Daily Mail* leader declared: 'Millions of us have seen interviewers adopt an aggressive attitude and hectoring tone as though the man or woman in the chair had committed some offence they wished to hide,' and referred to 'virtually defenceless people ... butchered to make a Roman holiday'. Yet the programme began inquiries, pursued by the press, that resulted in public exposure of the way Communists had infiltrated the Union's executive.

In 1958 Robin Day interviewed Harold Macmillan and asked him, 'How do you feel, Prime Minister, about criticism which has been made in the last few days, in Conservative newspapers particularly, of Mr Selwyn Lloyd, the Foreign Secretary?' Macmillan answered: 'I think Mr Selwyn Lloyd is a very good Foreign Secretary and has done his work extremely well. If I did not think so I would have made a change, but I do not intend to make a change simply as a result of pressure.'

Donald McLachlan wrote in the *Daily Telegraph*: 'Should the Prime Minister have been asked what he thought of his own Foreign Secretary before a camera that showed every flicker of the eyelid? Some say yes, some say no.' Cassandra (the late William Connor) said no. He wrote in the *Daily Mirror*: 'The Queen's First Minister was put on the spot. What else could he say about his colleague? How could he suddenly reject him? How could Mr Macmillan be anything but complimentary to his colleague? Mr Day, by his skill as an examiner, has been responsible for prolonging in office a man who probably doesn't want the job and is demonstrably incapable of doing it. The Idiot's Lantern is getting too big for its ugly gleam.'

Day had, in fact, asked a question that every journalist would have liked the opportunity to ask; the shock was simply that it was asked in front of a camera.

In 1962, when Britain was threatened with a national rail strike, the Minister of Transport was confronted with the General Secretary of the National Union of Railwaymen in a *Panorama* programme before they had sat down to negotiate officially in the conference chamber, and Richard Dimbleby, who chaired the programme, was accused of usurping the role of the Minister of Labour. But was television at fault in bringing face to face two men that every rail commuter earnestly wanted to get together?

It was in 1968, in two David Frost interview programmes, that television was widely felt to have gone too far. In one, Dr John Petro was confronted by drug addicts and doctors who questioned him about his prescriptions of drugs. In the second, Dr Emil Savundra, former head of an insurance company that had collapsed, was brought face to face with two widows with claims against the company and was booed by the studio audience. Both men were arrested shortly after the programmes (though the programme makers had not been aware that charges were imminent) and both were subsequently convicted of offences. A Labour MP, introducing an adjournment debate on 'the danger of television trials', likened the programmes to 'a lynch mob of the Wild West', and both the BBC and ITA gave assurances to the Postmaster-General that they would prevent 'television trials'. Consequently British television has never followed the example of television stations in Miami, Florida, where cameras have been concealed behind one-way mirrors to expose graft and where, for ten months in 1974, cameramen hid in vans and even a refrigerator packing-case to shoot film showing public officials, including a state attorney and a circuit court judge, hobnobbing with gamblers. Clandestine filming in Britain is rare.

Demonstrations

Coverage of demonstrations and protests has also caused criticism of television. There is an argument that if television did not cover demonstrations there would not be so many. America's Vice-President Spiro Agnew, in an onslaught in 1969 on US television newsmen, which they felt was intended to coerce them into attitudes more to the liking of President Nixon's administration, demanded, 'How many

Covering an anti-Vietnam war demonstration

marches and demonstrations would we have if the marchers did not know that the ever-faithful TV cameras would be there to record their antics for the next news show?'

Similar criticisms were heard in Britain. Edward Heath when Prime Minister interrupted a speech at Bristol in 1974 to blame a television crew for provoking a disturbance in the audience. The team had turned its lights and cameras on a group of heckling students. A scuffle broke out and one man threw his coat over a television camera to prevent it showing the Socialist literature being held up by the demonstrators. Heath snapped, 'It is the media, by turning their lights on part of the audience, which is causing this sort of disturbance.'

Yet television would be wrong to turn a blind eye to what happens. The BBC annual report of 1974 stated:

It is sometimes imagined that he who reports violence and anti-social conduct in general thereby endorses them. In many cases, those whose wrongdoing is exposed to public scrutiny by broadcasting are the more likely to be publicly repudiated. For example, during a royal visit to Stirling University, some members of the student body behaved discourteously to the Queen; they would be mistaken if they thought that the attention which journalists of the press, radio and television gave to their demonstration furthered the causes they claimed to have in mind.

Similarly, some viewers of film of the hostile behaviour of a few pickets towards non-strikers desiring to work imagined that the

This Week's *Peter Taylor (in glasses) reports on violence*

BBC was seeking to encourage that kind of militancy in industrial relations. In such situations each side wants the camera to function as an instrument of propaganda; in the hands of the professional journalist it must be only a tool of his craft.

A side effect of coverage of demonstrations was the desire of different parties to obtain television film for litigation. During the Scarman Inquiry into the Red Lion Square demonstration of 1974, in which a student died, ITN was required to produce not only the film it had screened but its untransmitted film. This was a matter of serious concern to ITN, not simply because untransmitted film is like the rough notes on a reporter's pad, but because if the films its cameramen are taking are liable to be used at a future date in prosecutions of either demonstrators or police, the cameramen will be in danger of becoming the first targets for violence. Both sides would have an interest in putting the camera out of action.

In 1975 there was a second case when Judge Claude Duveen heard a county court action in which two men and a woman claimed damages from the Chief Constable of Thames Valley for injuries they said they had suffered when police ejected fans from the site of a pop festival in Windsor Great Park. On this occasion ITN screened its transmitted film for the court but refused to produce the untransmitted film as the judge ordered. Nigel Ryan said at the time: 'We believe that the authority of ITN as a news broadcasting organization, and the ability of our reporting teams to gather news, depend on the public's confidence that ITN is solely concerned with the dissemination of news. This confidence may be undermined seriously if unused film material, which we regard as confidential, is always available to anybody for the purpose of litigation.'

ITN appealed against the judge's ruling and the Court of Appeal upheld the company. While it made clear that there was no general right to withhold news film when it was required by the course of justice, the court found that it had been oppressive to require the whole film to be shown when only one small incident was involved. Lord Denning, Master of the Rolls, said that the court respected the work of the journalist and would not hamper it more than necessary. Courts had the power to order the production of untransmitted film, but a judge should refuse the request if he considered it irrelevant or speculative. In other words, there were to be no 'fishing' expeditions in the hope of discovering evidence on the film.

Bias and space

From time to time partisans of one cause or another claim that television is biased against them, but television journalists strive hard to maintain impartiality. It is not always simple, even in the matter of political balance referred to in the last chapter. If a political leader makes news one day and there is no reply from the opposition, the television company cannot manufacture one. It must wait for a reply to restore the balance.

During the campaign before the 1975 referendum on Britain's membership of the EEC, balance was even more complex because pro- and anti-Common Market loyalties cut across normal party divisions; to give equal time to both sides the television companies literally resorted to stop-watches. And even then a moving camera has to be selectively directed – show a member of an audience yawning and the camera is editorializing. The wording of questions, designed to elicit information, can also be held to be editorializing. Yet Nigel Ryan points out: 'We have succeeded in reporting the situation in Northern Ireland over the past years with our programmes viewed in homes in Northern Ireland, in pubs in Southern Ireland and in army barracks in England and nobody has accused us of consistently slanting the news in one way or the other.'

This speaks highly for the editorial process for, as Alastair Burnet said in a lecture in 1970: *

* First Richard Spriggs Memorial Lecture.

'The very selection of the news involves bias. There is some bias in every programme about public policy; the selection of the policy to be discussed and of those to discuss it means bias and this can be made to appear very serious.

'But I do not think we should let ourselves be too confused. The question is really rather simple; it is whether the men and women concerned – it always comes down to people – seem to be actively engaged in putting more bias in, and that is their reputation, or whether they seem to be actively engaged in trying to get as much bias out as possible, and that is their reputation. So if you are one of those who genuinely fear that television is trying to put one over on you, the answer, I suggest, is not to call for rigid controls on all television of public affairs. That way you throw out the good with the bad, the fair with the unfair. The answer is to give the same mental attention to what you are told on the screen as you give to your morning newspaper. Be critical . . . protest selectively.'

Currently the biggest single problem which television newsmen face is not an external pressure but the internal one of presenting a truthful and useful picture of what is happening in the time available. Space has always been a problem. Television has been criticized in the past, and sometimes rightly, for attempting to settle the future of Europe in a six-minute discussion, trying to let fifty people give their views on inflation in fifty minutes or, on the other hand, restricting a debate to protagonists guaranteed to provide verbal punch-ups which make good television but generate more heat than light.

In the seventies the problem became more acute as a growing number of people in the industry itself began to query whether some of the information on television did not create a distorted impression by too narrow treatment. They claimed that the news might show a bomb outrage, current affairs programmes might show how a group of people were affected by it, but the circumstances that led up to it, the causes and the policies, would not be adequately covered. Ryan says:

'The answer is that is that we need more elbow-room. We don't any longer have quite as much as we need. *News at Ten* was designed in 1967 to provide room, not only for the nuclear warhead of the news, but to set it in its background and evaluate its meaning. What has happened since is that there has been a huge increase in all the means of communication including land-links, Eurovision, jet aircraft and satellites. It is now possible to receive pictures of Cambodia this morning, and the volume of pictures we have is so great that the headache we have every single night is how to cram everything in. We now need more elbow-room to be able to set the news in its context in order that we do not suffer from distortion through contraction.'

Chapter 15
The future

There will be an increase in the amount of time devoted to news and current affairs in the future. Most people engaged in television journalism are convinced of it and discussion of one-hour newscasts has already begun, though they are unlikely to be introduced until there is a fourth television channel, which will not be until after the Annan Committee on Broadcasting has reported. America's big three networks show at least ninety minutes of news in the early evening, and another half-hour late at night. NBC has, since 1974, carried news from 5 to 7.30 every evening – two and a half hours of information, comment and features, interrupted only by commercials. However, few viewers stay tuned in from beginning to end of this period. Most switch on and off, watching for perhaps twenty minutes. The programme is designed to cater for this and recycles the main points of the news at intervals. In Britain, though some viewers of *News at Ten* switch off at the half-way commercial break, most watch to the end. But if BBC and ITV started a two-hour news, or if they began prematurely an hour's news, it might create a wholly new situation with a smaller number of viewers. 'This would be not necessarily worse, but different, and has to be thought about,' says Nigel Ryan. 'If we had an hour's programme and an audience that dipped in, then every half-hour we might have to top up with the headlines again. What I would prefer to do would be to hold a unitary audience through the period.' So ITN would like to launch a three-quarter hour programme before extending to an hour.

Opinions differ about the content of a one-hour news. There are those who hold that a one-hour programme should complement an earlier, compact news and consist of little more than the headlines of the news followed by an analysis by a current affairs team. Some advocate this split operation because they believe that more than one editorial viewpoint would safeguard impartiality, while others see practical difficulties in a news organization handling the whole programme. Thames Television's John Edwards says:

'I don't think it is easy to mix news and current affairs and I think two separate bunches of people would be required because you cannot switch easily from one to another – from, say, the political news of the day to a background piece about it. Very few news reporters can sustain longer reports and it would not be easy to do a two and a half minute news story one week and a half-hour investigative piece the next. And would a one-hour news be one hour of the same, or would it be half an hour of news and half an hour of features with a punchy first half and a boring second half? ITN makes an occasional stab at current affairs with an extended story but it would be difficult to achieve a balanced programme.'

Nigel Ryan disagrees:

'I think what we want is a longer news. The suggestion that there should be an hour consisting of just short news headlines and the rest devoted to analysis by a current affairs division is a beguiling but totally misleading concept because, while all of us must support the thesis that news needs instant analysis and background if it is not to be misleading, it is wrong and absurd to go so far in the other direction that the actual news must be sacrificed. You cannot divorce the function of analysis from the function of presentation of the facts, and the idea that newsmen should come in with coal from the coal-face and that current affairs men should then come in and convert the coal into diamonds is wholly wrong in my view. It is only the news people who are capable of delivering the instant analysis because they are on the spot. They have got a man in Da Nang, or wherever, who knows what is going on there, and they have the technical means of getting instant pictures from the spot. Certainly the current affairs people can do weekly evaluations and do them extremely well and should continue to do so. But nightly evaluation, not only connected but actually interwoven with the presentation of information, must be done by one body.'

It should be understood that when British television journalists talk about evaluation and interpretation in news programmes they do not mean editorializing in the manner of commentators such as Eric Severeid in the United States. British television is obliged to be impartial; it must not present its own opinions as a newspaper can and does, and it is never likely to be allowed to do so until there are as many alternative news channels as there are alternative newspapers, which is not a foreseeable event. What television has to do is present and interpret the viewpoints of different factions. Nigel Ryan recalls:

'When *News at Ten* came into being people said, "By introducing opinion into news you will destroy the objectivity of your news." You would indeed, but what we do, in fact, is evaluate the news. Every night when there is a big political story Julian Haviland analyses its meaning and significance at the sort of length we have in mind for a longer programme, but at the moment we have to concertina the rest of the news to make room for it. In no way do we impugn our impartiality by this evaluation, and current affairs should have the same standards of objectivity and impartiality as news. We supply the public with the ingredients of major issues on which they make up their minds. Neither news nor current affairs has the right to tell them how to make up their minds.'

Experiments in news

From time to time a 'news only' channel has been mooted. Its likelihood is small, unless there are developments in cable television. Not much more can be done to increase the number of channels in Britain within the existing system of broadcasting, with its internationally crowded airwaves, except by the use of underground cable which can carry many more programmes than can be broadcast through the air. In 1973 the Cable Television Association published proposals which envisaged nine programme channels linked to every home, the first offering a choice of all locally receivable television stations, the others including an arts channel, an education channel and a local news channel. But the cost and time involved in creating a national cable network seem likely to preserve this ideal in the realm of dreams. And the broadcasting authorities are against it for fear that its development might damage the existing off-air television systems. They have more sympathy for local community television by cable.

Limited experiments in piped community television began in 1972 when the Minister of Posts and Telecommunications licensed a company to provide a service in Greenwich offering locally originated programmes of news and current affairs in addition to BBC and ITV programmes. Four more areas – Bristol, Swindon, Sheffield and Wellingborough – were allowed similar experimental services later, and more were intended to follow. They made a feature of local sporting events. But it appeared unlikely that the stations (which were not allowed to carry advertising) would ever be viable under the restrictions imposed on them. Permission to accept advertising in 1975 came too late to save four of the stations.

Other experiments in the seventies have been with news sheets displayed on television screens. The BBC system, called Ceefax, and the IBA system, called Oracle, are geared to the fact that the television signal received by a set in the home is not continual; there are gaps into which can be fed other information that can be decoded by a special apparatus. This would not provide conventional television pictures but could display simple visual messages like headlines of up to 120 words. The decoding apparatus could be built into new sets and existing sets could be adapted to receive the service. The viewer would push a button and dial a three-digit number for the fact sheet required, and that would appear in about fifteen seconds and remain on the screen as long as he wishes. Day or night he could get the latest news headlines, weather forecasts, stock exchange prices, road reports, sports results, programme details and other information. Test transmissions began in 1973 and the television news organizations geared themselves to supply material for this service. Technically there were no insuperable difficulties; the snag was again the capital expenditure involved.

Preparing a page for Ceefax

Money has also been concerning the producers of regular television news and current affairs programmes. The only costs which have shrunk in recent years have been those of satellite facilities. Costs of everything else from staff to transport have risen and placed some curbs on extending news coverage. Nevertheless, plans go on. The main technical change is likely to be the arrival of lightweight electronic cameras as portable as 16-mm film cameras and capable of delivering quality equal to that of big outside broadcast video cameras. American news companies are already equipping cameramen with small video cameras and back-pack video recorders, but British television men claim that our television picture is superior in quality to America's and wish to keep it that way, and they are not yet satisfied with the hardware available.

In presentation of the news there are likely to be few major changes. At one time it was widely thought that satellites would result in newscasters introducing programmes from Washington or Tokyo, or wherever the main news story was breaking. In actuality, although *News at Ten* has been introduced by Andrew Gardner from Paris and Reginald Bosanquet from Dublin, this makes little impression on the viewer; he still sees a man in a studio. And it is probable that many

ITN experimenting with portable television camera and back pack

viewers prefer to feel that the newscaster is in London linking correspondents around the world. Certainly television has moved on from
the pre-ITV days when news was read by a cipher in a suit, but no
British television men want to see the degree of personalization of
news adopted by one New York station, which features idiosyncratic
reporters and droll newscasters. Nor would they accept importing
sensationalism from another station which specializes in lurid crime
coverage. What does seem certain is that television will become, even
more than it is now, the public's first and main source of information.
The press will still have a role to play for, as the BBC's chairman, Sir
Michael Swann, said in a speech in 1975, the total content of *The
Times* would take between two and four days to deliver on television.
Even with longer news bulletins, television will remain a tabloid
medium giving only the chief facts.

Yet if people watched only television news they would still have a
good knowledge of the main happenings in the world. And since
viewers usually watch other programmes as well as the news, on current affairs, on the arts, on sport and on science, television gives them,
overall, a wide view of events. The change in television's role from an
entertainer to an entertainer and informer has taken place in an
extraordinarily short time.

Bibliography

Some books of the Seventies

Behind the Screen. The broadcasting memoirs of Lord Hill of Luton. Sidgwick & Jackson, 1974.

Day by Day. Robin Day. Kimber, 1975.

In and Out of the Box. Robert Dougall. Collins, 1973; Fontana, 1975.

ITV Evidence to the Annan Committee. Independent Television Publications, 1975.

The Mass Media. Stuart Hood. Macmillan, 1972.

The Ravenous Eye. Milton Shulman. Cassell, 1973; Coronet, 1975.

Richard Dimbleby. Jonathan Dimbleby. Hodder & Stoughton, 1975.

The Shadow in the Cave. A study of the relationship between the broadcaster, his audience and the state. Anthony Smith. Allen & Unwin, 1973.

Television News. Irving E. Fang. Hastings House, 1972.

To Kill a Messenger. Television news and the real world. William Small. Hastings House, 1970.

The Work of the Television Journalist. Robert Tyrrell. Focal Press, 1972.

A great many free brochures on aspects of television policy, technology and practice are published free by the IBA and BBC.

Acknowledgments

The publishers would like to thank the following for permission to reproduce the photographs in this book:

Associated Newspapers, page 96; *BBC Photograph Library*, pages 12, 22, 24, 31, 32, 33, 69, 81, 82, 86, 91, 93 (top), 94, 100, 103, 119 (top), 125, 139; *Granada Television*, pages 110, 112, 132; *ITN*, pages 46, 93 (bottom), 107, 114; *Keystone Press*, pages 20–21; *London Express News*, page 108; *London Weekend Television*, pages 15, 36; *Pacemaker Press*, page 133; *Popperfoto*, pages 37, 42–3, 126; *Press Association*, pages 53 (top), 87, 119 (bottom); *Roger Scruton*, pages 49, 53 (bottom), 61, 62, 63, 67, 76, 140; *Phil Sheldon, Blinkers*, page 129; *Southern Television*, pages 27, 101 (bottom), 102; *Syndication International*, page 73; *Thames Television*, pages 17, 88, 89, 101 (top), 123; *TVTimes*, pages 39, 44, 80.

Cover photograph showing Harold Wilson's resignation from premiership taken at No. 10 Downing Street by Malcolm Goy.

Index